Verbal Reasoning

Assessment Papers

10–11+ years

Book 2

Great Clarendon Street, Oxford, OX2 6DP, United Kingdom

Oxford University Press is a department of the University of Oxford. It furthers the University's objective of excellence in research, scholarship, and education by publishing worldwide. Oxford is a registered trade mark of Oxford University Press in the UK and in certain other countries

First published in 2015

This new edition 2020

British Library Cataloguing in Publication Data
Data available

978-0-19-277745-4

10 9 8 7 6 5 4

Paper used in the production of this book is a natural, recyclable product made from wood grown in sustainable forests.
The manufacturing process conforms to the environmental regulations of the country of origin.

Printed in China

Acknowledgements

The publishers would like to thank the following for permissions to use copyright material:

Page make-up: OKS Prepress, India
Cover illustrations: Lo Cole

Although we have made every effort to trace and contact all copyright holders before publication this has not been possible in all cases. If notified, the publisher will rectify any errors or omissions at the earliest opportunity.

Before you get started

What is Bond?

This book is part of the Bond Assessment Papers series for verbal reasoning, which provides a **thorough and progressive course in verbal reasoning** from ages six to twelve. It builds up verbal reasoning skills from book to book over the course of the series.

Bond's verbal reasoning resources are ideal preparation for the 11⁺ and other secondary school selection exams.

How does the scope of this book match real exam content?

Verbal Reasoning 10–11⁺ Book 1 and *Book 2* are the core Bond 11⁺ books. Each paper is **pitched at the level of a typical 11⁺ exam** and practises a wide range of questions drawn from the four distinct groups of verbal reasoning question types: sorting words, selecting words, anagrams, coded sequences and logic. The papers are fully in line with 11⁺ and other selective exams for this age group but are designed to practise **a wider variety of skills and question types** than most other practice papers so that children are always challenged to think – and don't get bored repeating the same question type again and again. We believe that variety is the key to effective learning. It helps children 'think on their feet' and cope with the unexpected: it is surprising how often children come out of verbal reasoning exams having met question types they have not seen before.

What does the book contain?

- **13 papers** – each one contains 80 questions.
- **Tutorial links throughout** – 📖 – this icon appears in the margin next to the questions. It indicates links to the relevant section in *How to do 11⁺ Verbal Reasoning*, our invaluable subject guide that offers explanations and practice for all core question types.
- **Scoring devices** – there are score boxes in the margins and a Progress Chart on page 60. The chart is a visual and motivating way for children to see how they are doing. It also turns the score into a percentage that can help you decide what to do next.
- **Next Steps Planner** – advice on what to do after finishing the papers can be found on the inside back cover.
- **Answers** – located in an easily-removed central pull-out section.

How can you use this book?

One of the great strengths of Bond Assessment Papers is their flexibility. They can be used at home, in school and by tutors to:

- set **timed formal practice tests** – allow about 45 minutes per paper in line with standard 11⁺ demands. Reduce the suggested time limit by five minutes to practise working at speed.

- provide **bite-sized chunks** for regular practice
- **highlight strengths and weaknesses** in the core skills
- identify **individual needs**
- set **homework**
- follow **a complete 11+ preparation strategy** alongside *The Parents' Guide to the 11+* (see below).

It is best to start at the beginning and work through the papers in order. If you are using the book as part of a careful run-in to the 11+, we suggest that you also have two other essential Bond resources close at hand:

Bond 11+ Verbal Reasoning Handbook: the subject guide that explains all the question types practised in this book. Use the cross-reference icons to find the relevant sections.

The Parents' Guide to the 11+: the step-by-step guide to the whole 11+ experience. It clearly explains the 11+ process, provides guidance on how to assess children, helps you to set complete action plans for practice and explains how you can use *Verbal Reasoning 10–11+ Book 1* and *Book 2* as part of a strategic run-in to the exam.

See the inside front cover for more details of these books.

What does a child's score mean and how can it be improved?

It is unfortunately impossible to guarantee that a child will pass the 11+ exam if they achieve a certain score on any practice book or paper. Success on the day depends on a host of factors, including the scores of the other children sitting the test. However, we can give some guidance on what a score indicates and how to improve it.

If children colour in the Progress Chart on page 60, this will give an idea of present performance in percentage terms. The Next Steps Planner inside the back cover will help you to decide what to do next to help a child progress. It is always valuable to go over wrong answers with children. If they are having trouble with any particular question type, follow the tutorial links to *How to do 11+ Verbal Reasoning* for step-by-step explanations and further practice.

Don't forget the website...!

Visit www.bond11plus.co.uk for lots of advice, information and suggestions on everything to do with Bond, the 11+ and helping children to do their best.

Paper 1

Find and underline the two words which need to change places for each sentence to make sense.

B 17

Example She went to letter the write.

1 The queue to the museum stood in the visitors.

2 Not had she packed any lunch.

3 Most bones like dogs.

4 I ran upstairs get to my book.

5 Out jumped he of the tree.

5

Underline one word in the brackets which is most opposite in meaning to the word in capitals.

B 6

Example	WIDE	(broad vague long narrow motorway)
6	APPEAR	(look image vanish seem arrival)
7	SILENT	(quiet shy peaceful noisy still)
8	RISE	(grow descend slope raise position)
9	PLAIN	(flat fancy simple ugly clear)
10	RUNNY	(flowing solid stream dashing liquid)

5

11–15 Look at these groups of words.

B 1

A	B	C	D
hamster	peach	tennis	cod
elephant	plum	cricket	haddock

Choose the correct group for each of the words below. Write in the letter.

trout ___	kiwi ___	rounders ___	cheetah ___	plaice ___
satsuma ___	weasel ___	salmon ___	lacrosse ___	badminton ___

5

Underline two words, one from each group, that go together to form a new word. The word in the first group always comes first.

B 8

Example (hand, green, for) (light, house, sure)

16 (moth, ant, frog) (hop, eater, tick)

17 (bottom, lap, write) (pencil, ink, top)

18 (more, make, need) (want, less, done)

19 (friend, sea, wreck) (best, kind, ship)

20 (fox, skip, broad) (den, cast, rope)

5

Underline the pair of words most similar in meaning.

Example	come, go	roam, wander	fear, fare
21	night, dawn	seldom, often	guess, suspect
22	hand, foot	option, choice	few, many
23	diminish, lessen	proceed, stop	absence, presence
24	near, far	ruler, controller	need, wish
25	dog, pet	solid, hollow	job, task

Aiden and Chloe like tennis.
Beth and Chloe like football, but not swimming.
Only Daxa likes tennis and swimming.

26 Which sport is most popular? ____________

If A = 2, B = 4, C = 5 and D = 6, give the answers to each of these calculations as a letter.

27 $(D - B) \times A =$ ___

28 $D + B - C =$ ___

29 $(A \times B) \div B =$ ___

Fill in the crosswords so that all the given words are included. You have been given one letter as a clue in each crossword.

30–31

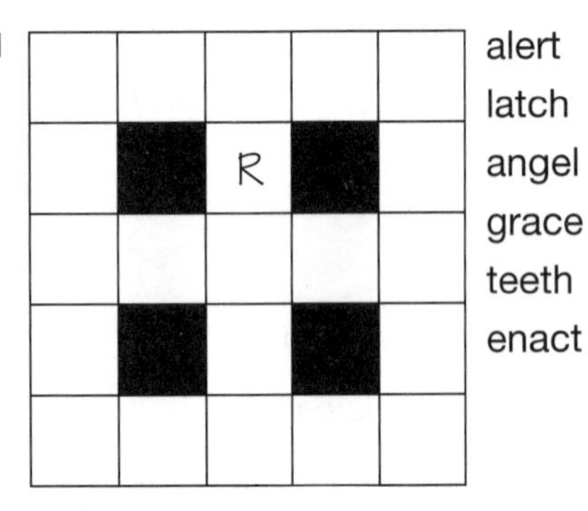

alert
latch
angel
grace
teeth
enact

32–33

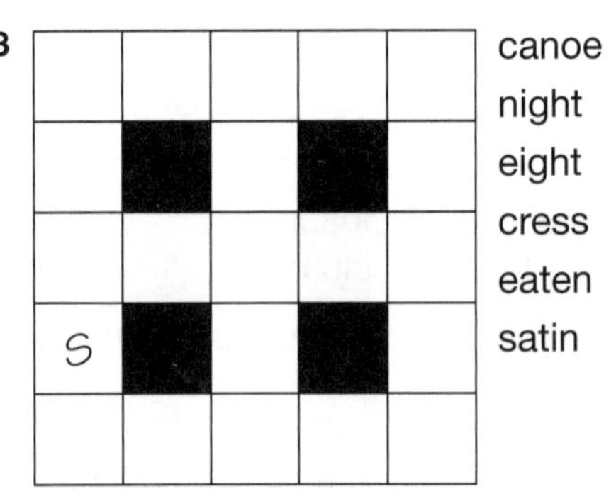

canoe
night
eight
cress
eaten
satin

Fill in the missing letters. The alphabet has been written out to help you.
A B C D E F G H I J K L M N O P Q R S T U V W X Y Z

Example AB is to CD as PQ is to <u>RS</u>.

34 CD is to EF as IJ is to ____.

35 FH is to HG as MO is to ____.

36 XV is to UY as JH is to ____.

37 RN is to SO as BD is to ____.

38 AD is to ZW as CF is to ____.

If * ^ % £ ! ^ ~ # is the code for H O M E W O R K, what are the codes for these words?

B 24

39 MORE ________

40 WORM ________

41 MEEK ________

42 WHERE ________

43 ROOM ________

5

Laura, Omar, James, Kate, Eva and Jacob are six children. Omar is older than Kate, but younger than Laura. James is the oldest child and Eva is not the youngest. Kate is older than just two children.

B 25

List the children in order of age, starting with the oldest.

44 ________

45 ________

46 ________

47 ________

48 ________

49 ________

6

Give the two missing numbers in the following sequences.

B 23

Example	2	4	6	8	10	12
50	16	13	17	___	___	15
51	3	6	12	___	___	96
52	2	3	5	___	8	___
53	7	___	12	16	21	___
54	5	1	10	___	___	3

5

Find the letter which will end the first word and start the second word.

B 10

Example peac (h) ome

55 pos (___) rip

56 wor (___) oan

57 war (___) haw

58 lic (___) ase

59 her (___) amp

5

Change the first word into the last word, by changing one letter at a time and making a new, different word in the middle.

Example CASE CASH LASH

60 STOP ______ STEM

61 LOVE ______ GIVE

62 JEER ______ DEAR

63 BAIT ______ PAIL

64 CRAB ______ GRUB

Underline the one word in the brackets which will go equally well with both the pairs of words outside the brackets.

Example rush, attack cost, fee (price, hasten, strike, charge, money)

65 regarding, concerning roughly, nearly (refer, close, about, almost, talking)

66 unlocked, unfastened start, launch (gaping, place, open, shut, begin)

67 break, crack bite, nip (quick, snap, twig, burst, sharp)

68 faded, dim collapse, black out (dizzy, light, sick, faint, dull)

69 annoyed, grumpy circle, square (shape, angry, cross, diamond, cut)

Read the first two statements and then underline one of the four options below that must be true.

70 'Chairs are furniture. Furniture can be made of wood.'

Trees supply wood.

Wood is used for all furniture.

Chairs can be made of wood.

Trees are furniture because they are wood.

Find the four-letter word hidden at the end of one word and the beginning of the next word. The order of the letters may not be changed.

Example The children had bats and balls. sand

71 If you blow and blow the candle will go out. ______

72 The argument began when Laurie took Jenna's phone. ______

73 Each opponent must weigh in first. ______

74 Will you help me find one that isn't broken? ______

75 The rabbits stayed quite still as we passed. ______

Underline the one word which **cannot be made** from the letters of the word in capital letters.

Example	STATIONERY	stone	tyres	ration	<u>nation</u>	noisy
76	DIGESTION	signet	onset	notice	tides	stone
77	INTENSIVE	tense	sieve	veins	events	nineteen
78	UNDERNEATH	tender	earth	turned	dated	heated
79	THURSDAY	shard	dusty	thuds	rusty	hurry
80	ANSWERED	swear	drawer	snared	swede	waned

5

Now go to the Progress Chart to record your score! Total 80

Paper 2

Give the two missing numbers in the following sequences.

Example	2	4	6	8	<u>10</u>	<u>12</u>
1	63	___	49	42	35	___
2	4	8	___	32	64	___
3	19	___	15	___	11	9
4	12	14	___	19	22	___
5	27	24	23	___	19	___

5

In 3 years' time Sarah will be twice as old as Emma was last year. Emma is now 11.

6 How old is Sarah now? ________

1

Here are the number codes for four words. Match the right word to the right code.

WALL	LAMP	MALE	PALE
5274	3255	4256	7256

7 WALL ________

8 LAMP ________

9 MALE ________

10 PALE ________

11 Write the code for LEAP. ________

5

Complete the following sentences in the best way by choosing one word from each set of brackets.

Example Tall is to (tree, short, colour) as narrow is to (thin, white, wide).

12 Horse is to (foal, stable, saddle) as cow is to (milk, grass, calf).

13 Car is to (petrol, speed, driver) as aeroplane is to (pilot, holiday, airport).

14 Hurry is to (hasten, slow, move) as assemble is to (school, repeat, gather).

15 Match is to (burn, stick, game) as head is to (hair, body, boss).

16 Spring is to (summer, season, jump) as march is to (calendar, walk, winter).

Rearrange the muddled letters in capitals to make a proper word. The answer will complete the sentence sensibly.

Example A BEZAR is an animal with stripes. ZEBRA

17 Look right and left before you SORCS the road. ________

18 Katie enjoyed her summer YHLADOI. ________

19 He used the LERUR to underline the title. ________

20 She hurt her STRIW. ________

21 The whole class went to the YAPTR. ________

Underline the one word in the brackets which will go equally well with both the pairs of words outside the brackets.

Example rush, attack cost, fee (price, hasten, strike, charge, money)

22 end, point empty, pour out (nib, spill, tip, rubbish, top)

23 bounce, leap leave out, miss (jump, try, ball, skip, forget)

24 guide, teach performance, act (parade, explain, show, amuse, lead)

25 location, area arrange, put (spot, flowers, live, place, keep)

26 document, folder note, store (notice, paper, file, remark, keep)

Find the missing number by using the two numbers outside the brackets in the same way as the other sets of numbers.

Example 2 [8] 4 3 [18] 6 5 [25] 5

27 5 [15] 10 7 [15] 8 3 [___] 13

28 6 [2] 4 15 [10] 5 12 [___] 8

29 12 [24] 2 9 [27] 3 8 [___] 5

30 6 [12] 5 4 [8] 3 12 [___] 2

31 13 [16] 3 12 [23] 11 8 [___] 17

Complete the following sentences by selecting the most sensible word from each group of words given in the brackets. Underline the words selected.

B 14

Example The (children, books, foxes) carried the (houses, books, steps) home from the (greengrocer, library, factory).

32 The (girl, puppy, toy) asked her (toy, mother, bone) for some (rain, shops, sweets).

33 Remember to (cross, ask, check) your (work, friend, breakfast) before handing it to the (dentist, teacher, waiter).

34 They enjoy (skipping, riding, swimming) their (horses, boats, fish) in the (playground, field, pitch).

35 Mix the (bowl, butter, kitchen) with the (sugar, mustard, medicine), then add some (detergent, powder, eggs).

36 The weather was (foggy, sunny, frosty) and too (easy, moody, hot) to play on the (beach, circus, cinema).

5

Underline two words, one from each group, that go together to form a new word. The word in the first group always comes first.

B 8

Example (hand, green, for) (light, house, sure)

37 (small, cross, draw) (shout, shape, roads)

38 (share, cap, telephone) (size, cause, ring)

39 (use, beauty, me) (full, less, all)

40 (grass, sea, shine) (sun, bright, weed)

41 (go, near, walk) (close, far, by)

5

Move one letter from the first word and add it to the second word to make two new words.

B 13

Example hunt sip *hut* *snip*

42 climb rack ________ ________

43 forty part ________ ________

44 splay crumb ________ ________

45 ruin deal ________ ________

46 thrust sore ________ ________

5

Underline the two words, one from each group, which are closest in meaning.

B 3

Example (race, shop, start) (finish, begin, end)

47 (calm, sea, cool) (wind, still, waves)

48 (sun, beam, star) (hot, shine, sky)

49 (dog, scratch, claw) (graze, knee, sore)

50 (fair, rich, dark) (poor, honest, reliable)

51 (hit, fall, force) (hand, power, fail)

5

Find the letter which will end the first word and start the second word.

Example peac (h) ome

52 note (__) eaf   53 jump (__) hape

54 rai (__) aft   55 kne (__) ide

56 fro (__) lee

Find the three-letter word which can be added to the letters in capitals to make a new word. The new word will complete the sentence sensibly.

Example The cat sprang onto the MO. USE

57 He ate fish and CS in the café. ______

58 The NOT appeared in the newspaper. ______

59 I helped my mother with the SPING. ______

60 Try to LN your spellings in time for the test. ______

61 The car SPED at the traffic lights. ______

Fill in the crosswords so that all the given words are included. You have been given one letter as a clue in each crossword.

62–63

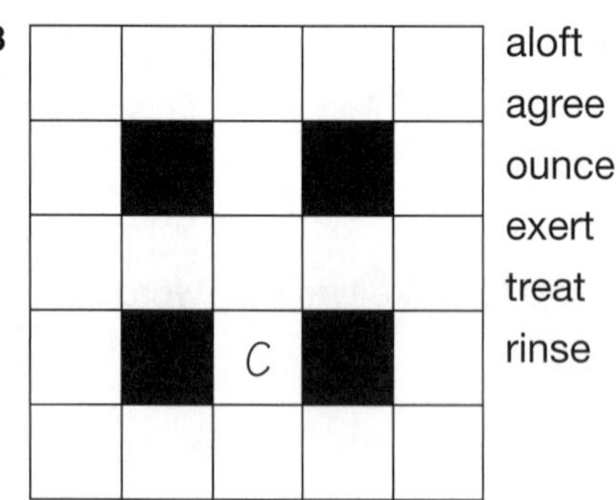

aloft
agree
ounce
exert
treat
rinse

64–65

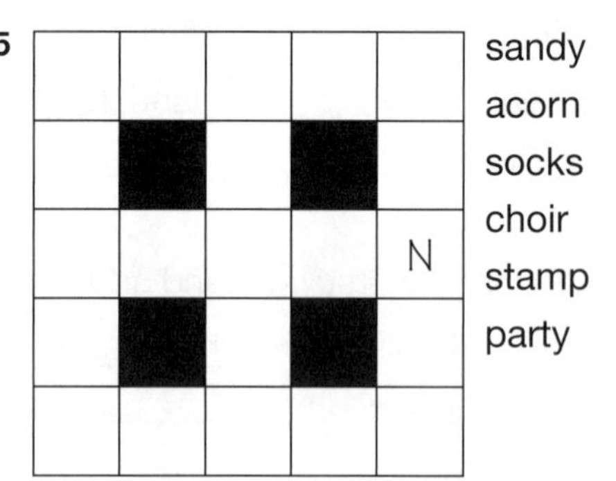

sandy
acorn
socks
choir
stamp
party

Give the two missing groups of letters in the following sequences. The alphabet has been written out to help you.

A B C D E F G H I J K L M N O P Q R S T U V W X Y Z

Example	CQ	DP	EQ	FP	GQ	HP
66	ZA	____	XC	WD	____	UF
67	CA	EC	GE	IG	____	____
68	VAJ	WBK	XCL	YDM	____	____
69	AT	DR	____	JN	____	PJ
70	PA	BQ	RC	DS	____	____

If P = 6, Q = 4, R = 2, S = 12 and T = 8, give the answer to each of these calculations as a letter.

B 26

71 $P + Q + R =$ ___ **72** $(Q \times Q) - (P - R) =$ ___

73 $Q \times R =$ ___ **74** $S \div R =$ ___

75 $(R \times T) \div Q =$ ___

5

Which one letter can be added to the front of all of these words to make new words?

B 12

Example	care	cat	crate	call
76 ___owl	___one	___reak	___ray	___rain
77 ___am	___oint	___ump	___ust	___ewel
78 ___ront	___oil	___lower	___orce	___ool
79 ___ake	___ait	___eed	___ild	___hat
80 ___ear	___ame	___eigh	___est	___ose

5

Now go to the Progress Chart to record your score! **Total** 80

Paper 3

Look at these groups of words.

B 1

A	B	C
Trees	Food	Birds

Choose the correct group for each of the words below. Write in the letter.

1–5 parrot ___ pine ___ broccoli ___ willow ___ eagle ___

beans ___ noodles ___ wren ___ robin ___ oak ___

5

Underline the two words which are the odd ones out in the following groups of words.

B 4

Example	black	king	purple	green	house
6	idea	thought	clever	notion	dull
7	divide	join	subtract	unite	combine
8	nearby	remote	neighbouring	foreign	distant
9	compel	lively	force	pressure	sad
10	hint	lie	complaint	sign	indication

5

Find the letter which will end the first word and start the second word.

B 10

Example peac (h) ome

11 mos (___) alt

12 jum (___) lum

13 gla (___) eck

14 sol (___) nion

15 win (___) nit

5

Complete the following sentences by selecting the most sensible word from each group of words given in the brackets. Underline the words selected.

B 14

Example The (children, books, foxes) carried the (houses, books, steps) home from the (greengrocer, library, factory).

16 We all need (books, food, soap) to help build a (healthy, cold, solid) (garden, air, body).

17 A (lion, giraffe, crocodile) can eat the (leaves, rice, meat) from the (highest, fastest, tidiest) part of the tree.

18 Never (fly, sing, stand) under a (tree, bird, aeroplane) during a thunderstorm.

19 He left after (lunch, breakfast, midnight) on a (rainy, summery, hot) November (year, night, Christmas).

20 She (cried, asked, whispered) her (dog, toy, mother) before using her new (computer, walk, house).

5

Underline the pair of words most opposite in meaning.

B 9

Example	cup, mug	coffee, milk	hot, cold
21	danger, risk	notice, remark	guilty, innocent
22	exact, true	slow, swift	connect, link
23	joy, sorrow	uncover, open	mistake, error
24	floppy, hanging	hazard, safety	alike, same
25	accurate, wrong	roomy, spacious	lap, circuit

5

Complete the following expressions by filling in the missing word.

B 15

Example Pen is to ink as brush is to paint.

26 Mother is to father as ________________ is to son.

27 Century is to hundred as dozen is to ________________.

28 Find is to fine as mind is to ________________.

29 Flock is to sheep as ________________ is to cows.

30 January is to December as Tuesday is to ________________.

5

Find a word that can be put in front of each of the following words to make new, compound words.

B 11

Example	cast	fall	ward	pour	down
31	boat	buoy	guard	jacket	______
32	gap	over	watch	page	______
33	guard	fighter	fly	power	______
34	work	land	pecker	worm	______
35	ache	stroke	ward	date	______

5

Underline the one word in the brackets which will go equally well with both the pairs of words outside the brackets.

B 5

Example	rush, attack	cost, fee	(price, hasten, strike, charge, money)
36	ice, chill	stop, standstill	(cold, fix, freeze, wintry, halt)
37	team, gang	edge, margin	(party, side, limit, area, support)
38	boring, uninteresting	gloomy, cloudy	(clear, weather, exciting, dull, work)
39	here, attending	gift, donation	(guest, charity, ready, present, show)
40	find, hunt	path, trail	(train, track, sniff, catch, line)

5

Thomas, Kasim, Charlotte and Elena all have sandwiches in their lunchboxes.
Most of the children prefer healthy snacks.
Elena has a pear and Kasim has an apple.
Thomas, Charlotte and Elena have yogurts.
Elena was running late for school and is the only child who has forgotten to bring a drink.
Kasim has a snack bar in case he still feels hungry.

B 25

41 How many children have sandwiches, yogurt and a drink for lunch? ______

42 Which two children have the same items for lunch? ______

43 Which child has the most items in their lunchbox? ______

3

Fill in the crosswords so that all the given words are included. You have been given one letter as a clue in each crossword.

B 19

44–45

	I				

stamps, angers, disuse, nested, extend, timber

46–47

			L		

messed, prised, antler, pilots, inside, floods

4

If < £ > < / ? $ £ is the code for SENSIBLE what do these codes stand for?

B 24

48 < £ > < £ ______

49 $ / > £ ______

50 $ £ < < ______

What are the codes for the following words?

51 BINS ______

52 BLISS ______

5

Give the two missing numbers in the following sequences.

B 23

Example	2	4	6	8	10	12
53	17	21	___	29	___	37
54	15	___	20	18	___	27
55	96	48	24	12	___	___
56	47	___	41	38	35	___
57	14	23	33	___	56	___

5

modem monster model mould mobile

If these words were placed in alphabetical order, which word would come:

B 20

58 second? ______

59 last? ______

60 first? ______

3

Find the four-letter word hidden at the end of one word and the beginning of the next word. The order of the letters may not be changed.

B 21

Example The children had bats and balls. sand

61 Sometimes I wash old golf balls then resell them. ______

62 Some of the buses went on but mine stopped at the corner. ______

63 We are going to paint your room this weekend. ______

64 The missing cat eventually came home. ______

65 Everyone at my office begins at nine. ______

5

Rearrange the muddled letters in capitals to make a proper word. The answer will complete the sentence sensibly.

B 16

Example A BEZAR is an animal with stripes. ZEBRA

66–67 They climbed the ERET at the TTMOOB of the garden. ______ ______

68 Dark clouds usually bring IANR. ______

69–70 Switch your THILG off by NENI. ______ ______

5

Underline the one word which **cannot be made** from the letters of the word in capital letters.

B 7

Example STATIONERY stone tyres ration <u>nation</u> noisy

71	DESCRIPTION	cried	snort	nicer	pride	preen
72	BREAKDOWN	brand	wander	dream	rowed	brown
73	PLASTERING	staring	string	laser	grass	strain
74	BANNISTER	banter	stern	nasty	rinse	tribe
75	SILHOUETTE	house	those	teeth	heels	honest

5

Find the three-letter word which can be added to the letters in capitals to make a new word. The new word will complete the sentence sensibly.

B 22

Example The cat sprang onto the MO. USE

76 On Saturday they went to the nursery to buy some PLS. ______

77 She only managed to write a couple of SENCES. ______

78 Take that out of your MH! ______

79 The mobile phone TERY was low. ______

80 SHAR your pencils please. ______

5

Now go to the Progress Chart to record your score! Total 80

Paper 4

Underline two words, one from each group, that go together to form a new word. The word in the first group always comes first.

B 8

Example (hand, <u>green</u>, for) (light, <u>house</u>, sure)

1 (birthday, card, best) (week, fun, board)

2 (we, his, my) (sister, self, own)

3 (no, yes, nice) (thanks, there, thing)

4 (bread, butter, knife) (cup, fork, spread)

5 (rug, mat, go) (door, by, stick)

5

Add one letter to the word in capital letters to make a new word. The meaning of the new word is given in the clue.

B 12

Example PLAN simple plain

6 PIECE make a hole ____________

7 FIN not rainy ____________

8 ONE on one occasion ____________

9 LOSE unfastened ____________

10 MAN unkind ____________

5

Underline the one word in the brackets which will go equally well with both the pairs of words outside the brackets.

B 5

Example rush, attack cost, fee (price, hasten, strike, charge, money)

11 club, diamond hoe, rake (weapon, spade, jewel, garden, heart)

12 bracelet, necklace telephone, bell (wedding, ring, line, valuable, rich)

13 toss, throw actors, players (grab, role, project, catch, cast)

14 cosy, at ease well-off, wealthy (easy, rich, comfortable, helpful, happy)

15 decrease, reduce ignore, unimportant (share, sale, allow, discount, bother)

5

Underline the two words which are the odd ones out in the following groups of words.

B 4

Example black king purple green house

16 run trainer walk sock jog

17 hot roast grill spicy toast

18 plan idea organize drawing prepare

19 cub cat gosling lamb goat

20 orange brown grass lemon cherry

5

Alice catches the bus at 7:15 am and arrives at her destination 1 hour 30 minutes later.

Her journey takes twice as long as Grace's.

Lucy's bus leaves at 7:45 am and her journey takes 20 minutes.

Grace's bus leaves at 7:30 am.

B 25

21 At what time does Alice complete her journey? ____________

22 At what time does Grace's bus reach its destination? ____________

23 At what time does Lucy's journey end? ____________

3

Give the two missing numbers in the following sequences. B 23

Example 2 4 6 8 10 12

24 17 ___ ___ 23 25 27

25 11 14 ___ ___ 33 18

26 ___ 4 6 9 13 ___

27 19 22 24 ___ ___ 32

28 ___ 5 3 ___ 4 15

5

Find the three-letter word which can be added to the letters in capitals to make a new word. The new word will complete the sentence sensibly. B 22

Example The cat sprang onto the MO. USE

29 She FED her mug with tea. ___________

30 When it's hot, my dog lies in the SE. ___________

31 Children usually prefer SY beaches. ___________

32 SUDLY, I wanted to go. ___________

33 The book is on the SH. ___________

5

Underline the pair of words most opposite in meaning. B 9

Example cup, mug coffee, milk hot, cold

34 forest, wood true, false, mild, gentle

35 student, pupil car, auto rear, front

36 visit, call cheeky, polite child, infant

37 allow, deny marry, join dig, burrow

38 change, swap same, alike total, partial

5

Find the letter which will end the first word and start the second word. B 10

Example peac (h) ome

39 luc (___) iss

40 bul (___) ell

41 gro (___) asp

42 fol (___) erb

43 oa (___) race

5

Read the first two statements and then underline one of the four options below that must be true. B 25

44 'Fish breathe underwater. Goldfish are a common type of pet fish.'

Goldfish make good pets.

The seas are full of fish.

Goldfish breathe underwater.

Fish live in salt water.

Read the first two statements and then underline one of the four options below that must be true.

45 'Bees make honey. Honey tastes sweet.'

Bees are sweet.

Everyone likes honey.

Bees make sweet honey.

Bees can sting.

Read the first two statements and then underline one of the four options below that must be true.

46 'Some shoes are made from leather. Leather is waterproof.'

Shoes are worn with socks.

All shoes are made from leather.

Leather shoes are waterproof.

Leather is the best material for shoes.

3

Fill in the crosswords so that all the given words are included. You have been given one letter as a clue in each crossword.

B 19

47–48

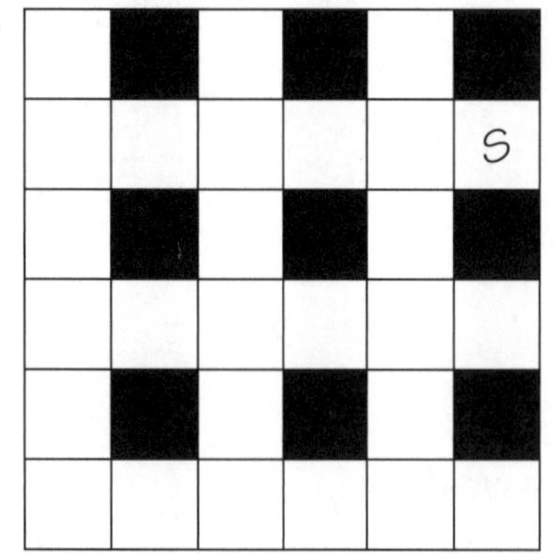

better, cheeky, trying, yogurt, exists, hordes

49–50

litter, glides, recede, strain, drawer, sunset

4

Fill in the missing letters. The alphabet has been written out to help you.

B 23

A B C D E F G H I J K L M N O P Q R S T U V W X Y Z

Example AB is to CD as PQ is to RS.

51 CN is to DO as HR is to ______.

52 HF is to JD as MW is to ______.

53 CBE is to DAF as PNS is to ______.

54 BD is to EG as RT is to ______.

55 LCF is to KBE as TXQ is to ______.

5

knead knight knick kneeing kneecap

B 20

If these words were put in alphabetical order, which one would come:

56 third? ________

57 fourth? ________

If the words were listed in reverse in alphabetical order, which one would come:

58 first? ________

59 last? ________

60 fourth? ________

5

If ? & $ * ! £ @ > < is the code for COMPUTERS, what do these codes stand for?

B 24

61 < £ & > @ ________

62 $ & < £ ________

63 ? & ! > < @ ________

What are the codes for the following words?

64 TERM ________

65 CUTE ________

5

Underline the two words which are made from the same letters.

B 7

	Example	TAP	PET	TEA	POT	EAT
66	NAME	AMEND	DREAM	MEAN	MADE	NEAR
67	TAPS	STARE	SNAP	TAPE	PANT	PANS
68	MILLS	MILES	SLIME	SAWN	WARM	WORM
69	MARCH	CHANT	WEAR	CHARM	WATCH	MARSH
70	SEVEN	PHRASE	SHAPE	GRAPH	PHASE	SEVER

5

Find and underline the two words which need to change places for each sentence to make sense.

B 17

Example She went to letter the write.

71 Dad drives to us school in the car.

72 She had knee her cut badly.

73 I have to wait and sit.

74 Mum knows we trick planning to were her.

75 We cash to the bank to get some went.

5

If s = 3, e = 2, r = 5, a = 1, t = 6 and d = 4, find the value of the following words by adding the letters together.

B 26

76 rested ________

77 read ________

78 treat ________

79 stared ________

80 deer ________

5

Now go to the Progress Chart to record your score! Total 80

Paper 5

Remove one letter from the word in capital letters to leave a new word. The meaning of the new word is given in the clue.

B 12

Example AUNT an insect <u>ant</u>

1 DOZEN sleep ________

2 TIRED joined ________

3 SPOUT place ________

4 BOUND connection ________

5 PLEASANT bumpkin ________

5

Underline the two words, one from each group, which are closest in meaning.

B 3

Example (race, shop, <u>start</u>) (finish, <u>begin</u>, end)

6 (hit, punch, hand) (success, fail, nervous)

7 (behave, complication, rule) (quiz, mood, problem)

8 (cheap, price, buy) (fee, purse, sell)

9 (mind, real, imagine) (eye, suppose, copy)

10 (test, proof, try) (lies, tell, evidence)

5

Find the missing number by using the two numbers outside the brackets in the same way as the other sets of numbers.

B 23

Example 2 [8] 4 3 [18] 6 5 [25] 5

11 9 [47] 5 3 [8] 2 12 [____] 3

12 12 [2] 6 81 [9] 9 24 [____] 12

13 13 [30] 12 12 [29] 12 7 [____] 12

14 9 [4] 4 7 [2] 4 10 [____] 4

15 16 [32] 2 8 [24] 3 7 [____] 3

5

Find the letter which will complete both pairs of words, ending the first word and starting the second. The same letter must be used for both pairs of words.

B 10

Example mea (t) able fi (t) ub

16 tria (____) ead rea (____) ight

17 pla (____) es tr (____) ellow

18 brin (____) host ran (____) rim

19 bul (____) lack cri (____) ald

20 foo (____) emper sal (____) hank

5

Underline the one word in the brackets which will go equally well with both the pairs of words outside the brackets.

B 5

Example rush, attack cost, fee (price, hasten, strike, charge, money)

21 practise, rehearse dig, pierce (roll, drill, wind, turn, study)

22 oar, pole dabble, splash (steer, wade, waves, paddle, river)

23 review, inspect stop, limit (examine, check, confirm, halt, accept)

24 explode, roar success, growth (thunder, echo, boom, crash, strong)

25 strength, energy make, cause (power, force, health, encourage, require)

5

Underline the one word which **cannot be made** from the letters of the word in capital letters.

B 7

Example STATIONERY stone tyres ration nation noisy

26 TELEPHONES shone pole photo honest spent

27 STATUES astute suet uses sauce states

28 PETRIFIES fires feast spite trees rites

29 CHRISTMAS smith chasm match charm start

30 RADISHES shade rashes dress shares drains

5

Find a word that is similar in meaning to the word in capital letters and that rhymes with the second word.

B 5

Example CABLE tyre *wire*

31 APPLAUD strap ______

32 ORDINARY train ______

33 BANQUET least ______

34 EMPLOY choir ______

35 LONGING burn ______

5

Find the four-letter word hidden at the end of one word and the beginning of the next word. The order of the letters may not be changed.

B 21

Example The children had bats and balls. *sand*

36 The clock struck twelve and minutes later we left. ______

37 The best emeralds are used for jewellery. ______

38 Some of his ideas were a bit unusual. ______

39 Some people find it hard to admit when they are wrong. ______

40 We made sure that no one missed their turn. ______

5

Change the first word into the last word by changing one letter at a time and making a new, different word in the middle.

B 13

Example CASE *CASH* LASH

41 WILL ______ WIND

42 PITH ______ WISH

43 HALL ______ SALT

44 OXEN ______ EVEN

45 KIND ______ BAND

5

Complete the following expressions by underlining the missing word.

B 15

Example Frog is to tadpole as swan is to (duckling, baby, cygnet).

46 Nimble is to agile as calm is to (excited, violent, still).

47 Soothe is to disturb as enjoy is to (adore, dislike, appreciate).

48 Grim is to pleasant as numerous is to (many, numbers, sparse).

49 Pleased is to delighted as greet is to (card, ignore, welcome).

50 Seldom is to often as descend is to (go, arrive, rise).

5

Fill in the crosswords so that all the given words are included. You have been given one letter as a clue in each crossword.

B 19

51–52

■		■		■	
■		■		■	
■		■		■	
		M			

simple, arrive, temple, cement
preens, aspect

53–54

■		■		■	
		V			
■		■		■	
■		■		■	

adders, reveal, revert, revere
styles, beheld

55–56

■		■		■	
■		■		■	
				O	
■		■		■	

nation, active, octave, finish
leaner, tether

6

Give the two missing numbers in the following sequences.

B 23

Example		2	4	6	8	10	12
57	16	20	25	___	34	38	___
58	___	64	56	___	40	32	24
59	85	___	61	52	___	40	37
60	6	___	12	20	18	30	___

4

A B C D E F G H I J K L M N O P Q R S T U V W X Y Z

Solve the problems by working out the letter codes.

B 24

61 If the code for BEAT is CFBU, what is the code for MICE? ________

62 If the code for TEST is VGUV, what is the code for JUMP? ________

63 If the code for SKATE is RJZSD, what is the code for LINE? ________

64 If the code for CONSIDER is AMLQGBCP, what does the code NSPQC stand for? ________

65 If the code for ALTER is BMUFS, what does the code ZPVOH stand for? ________

5

If A = 2, B = 4, C = 5, D = 10 and E = 8, give the answers to these calculations as letters.

66 B + E − A = ___

67 D × A ÷ B = ___

68 (E + B) − D = ___

69 C × A = ___

70 (D − B) + (E ÷ B) = ___

71 (B × A) − (A × A) = ___

6

Tom's hamster is 7 years younger than his cat. His dog, who is twice the age of the hamster, will be 7 next year.

72 How old is Tom's cat? __________

1

73 Write the letters of the word TADPOLE in the order in which they appear in the dictionary.

___ ___ ___ ___ ___ ___ ___

1

74 If the letters in the following word are arranged in alphabetical order, which letter comes in the middle?

MOVED ___

1

75 If the months of the year were arranged in alphabetical order, which month would come third?

____

1

Imagine each of these words spelled backwards, then write the number below each word to indicate if it would be 1st, 2nd, 3rd or 4th in alphabetical order.

76	taught	thought	naughty	daughter
	________	________	________	________
77	suit	fruit	juice	nuisance
	________	________	________	________
78	fabulous	anxious	famous	enormous
	________	________	________	________
79	illness	happiness	fitness	clumsiness
	________	________	________	________
80	terrible	squirrel	horrible	wheel
	________	________	________	________

5

Now go to the Progress Chart to record your score! **Total** 80

Paper 6

Give the two missing pairs of letters in the following sequences. The alphabet has been written out to help you.

B 23

A B C D E F G H I J K L M N O P Q R S T U V W X Y Z

Example	CQ	DP	EQ	FP	GQ	HP
1 ML	___	IH	GF	___	CB	
2 BC	DI	GN	___	PU	___	
3 AZ	___	EV	___	IR	KP	
4 KL	JM	___	HO	GP	___	
5 ZY	AB	XW	CD	___	___	

5

Fill in the crosswords so that all the given words are included. You have been given one letter as a clue in each crossword.

B 19

6–7

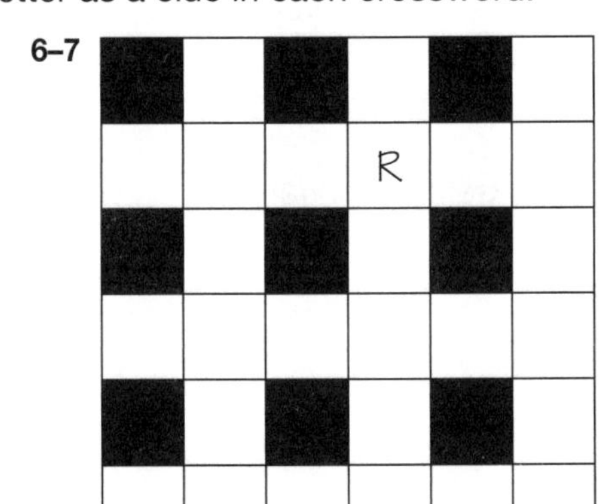

bearer, graded, eloped, triple, teller, friend

8–9

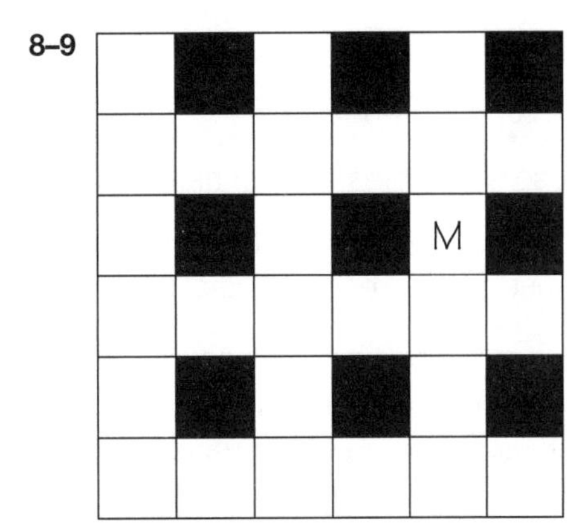

assume, banana, avenue, immune, ushers, answer

10–11

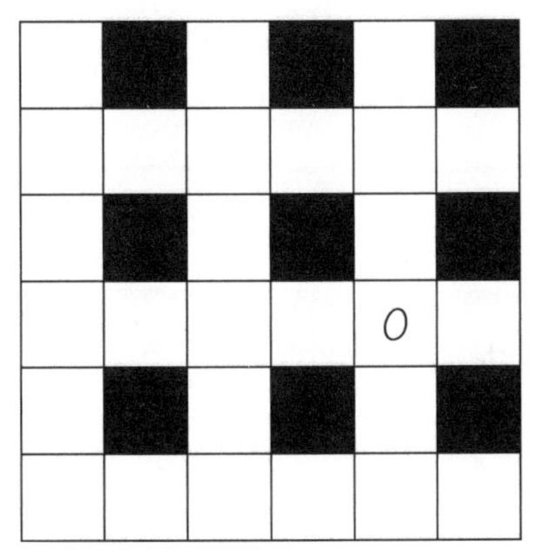

sunset, become, angles, needed, season, lesson

6

Find two letters which will end the first word and start the second word.

B 10

Example rea (c h) air

12 nett (__ __) opard

13 roa (__ __) ing

14 form (__ __) rand

15 glo (__ __) ware

16 opti (__ __) ion

5

Complete the following sentences by selecting the most sensible word from each group of words given in the brackets. Underline the words selected.

B 14

Example The (children, books, foxes) carried the (houses, books, steps) home from the (greengrocer, library, factory).

17 It was my (turn, problem, behaviour) to (swim, ride, walk) the (car, bike, trampoline).

18 We (picked, said, made) some (bread, strawberries, jam) in the (sand, river, field).

19 Please (wet, dry, dust) the (furniture, flowers, plates) before putting them in the (cupboard, case, wardrobe).

20 Wearing (trousers, goggles, boots) helps you to (swim, ride, trek) underwater.

21 I had to (complain, wonder, lie) about the (pleasant, exciting, loud) (treat, music, money) because it was keeping me awake.

5

Find the four-letter word hidden at the end of one word and the beginning of the next word. The order of these letters may not be changed.

B 21

Example The children had bats and balls. sand

22 Amy immediately posted her cards as she addressed them. ________

23 William, please come at once. ________

24 The sunset bathed the mountain in golden light. ________

3

Underline the pair of words most similar in meaning.

B 5

Example	come, go	roam, wander	fear, fare
25	rapid, slow	hide, seek	abundant, plentiful
26	rare, common	answer, reply	prize, punishment
27	transcend, translate	nothing, everything	rhythm, beat
28	alter, change	lead, follow	protect, attack
29	costly, cheap	injury, damage	famous, unknown

5

Hannah and Charlie live in the country.
Charlie and Raj like going to the cinema.
Raj and Daisy live in a town and go to Drama Club.

B 25

30 Who lives in a town and likes going to the cinema? ________

1

If the code for PREVIOUS is 79643582, what do these codes stand for?

B 24

31 2896 ________

32 78926 ________

33 9576 ________

34 If the code for PRETEND is TUVWVYZ, what is the code for RENT? ________

35 If the code for SHADE is 24536, what word is 4653? ________

5

If S = 3, E = 2, R = 5, A = 1, T = 6 and D = 4, find the value of the following.

B 26

36 $T + E + A =$ ________

37 $(R \times E) + (S \times T) =$ ________

38 $(S + T) - (A \times R) =$ ________

39 $(S \times E) \div (A \times T) =$ ________

40 Find the value of DRESSER by adding the letters together. ________

5

Find the three-letter word which can be added to the letters in capitals to make a new word. The new word will complete the sentence sensibly.

B 22

Example The cat sprang onto the MO. USE

41 My PNTS encourage me to play outside. ________

42–43 I packed lots of warm CLOS, but forgot my SPERS so my feet were cold.

________ ________

44–45 The GES were fine but the bananas hadn't yet RIED. ________ ________

5

Underline the word in the brackets closest in meaning to the word in capitals.

B 5

Example UNHAPPY (unkind death laughter sad friendly)

46 COLLECTION (hobby scrapbook assortment interesting valuable)

47 COACH (trip driver school child instructor)

48 EXTERIOR (paint fence inside outside private)

49 STABLE (horses hay wobbly fixed shaky)

50 MIX (divide cake blend fork icing)

5

Change the first word into the last word by changing one letter at a time and making two new, different words in the middle.

B 13

Example	TEAK	TEAT	TENT	RENT
51	CALM	______	______	POLE
52	LARK	______	______	HAZE
53	WAIT	______	______	JARS
54	SITE	______	______	BILL
55	DOZE	______	______	MADE

5

Change one word so that the sentence makes sense. Underline the word you are taking out and write your new word on the line.

B 14

Example I waited in line to buy a book to see the film. ticket

56 You should always wear a safety cap when riding a bicycle. ______

57 She put her car in the garden every night. ______

58 Copy the poem again; your trying isn't neat enough. ______

59 The moon was shining by midday, so he ate his lunch in the garden. ______

60 We sit in the garden until dark during the long days of winter. ______

5

Move one letter from the first word and add it to the second word to make two new words.

B 13

Example	hunt	sip	hut	snip
61	through	fog	______	______
62	boat	muse	______	______
63	tray	hem	______	______
64	blend	back	______	______
65	cheat	last	______	______

5

Find a word that can be put in front of each of the following words to make new, compound words.

B 11

Example	cast	fall	ward	pour	down
66	skirts	side	line	burst	______
67	on	date	roar	set	______
68	go	take	line	growth	______
69	spoon	cake	time	cup	______
70	box	card	code	age	______

5

Which word in each group contains only the first six letters of the alphabet?

Example	defeat	farce	abide	deaf	dice
71	badge	deck	bead	beach	fake
72	cage	deal	cake	fade	beak
73	ease	debacle	decade	fable	each
74	cuff	bean	calf	bake	café
75	edge	fail	face	feel	elf

B 18

5

Look at these groups of words.

A	B	C
Clothing	Coast	Calendar

B 1

Choose the correct group for each of the words below. Write in the letter.

76–79 sand ____ diving ____ linen ____ cliffs ____

era ____ waistcoat ____ annual ____ monday ____

4

Read the first two statements and then underline one of the four options below that must be true.

B 25

80 'A monkey is an animal. Some monkeys live in the rainforests.'

Most monkeys live in rainforests.

A rainforest is a hot place.

Some animals live in rainforests.

Monkeys climb trees.

1

Now go to the Progress Chart to record your score! **Total** 80

Paper 7

PROVOKE PROVINCE PROSPER PROVISION PROSPECT

B 20

If these words were placed in alphabetical order, which one would come:

1 first? ____________

2 last? ____________

3 middle? ____________

4 fourth? ____________

5 second? ____________

5

Underline one word in the brackets which is most opposite in meaning to the word in capitals.

B 6

Example WIDE (broad vague long narrow motorway)

6 STALE (bread crisp tasteless flat boring)

7 SPEAKER (teacher lawyer politician listener leader)

8 BUSY (active routine idle occupied service)

9 EXTEND (build reach shorten amount line)

10 BREAK (divide limb news connect fracture)

5

Find the three-letter word which can be added to the letters in capitals to make a new word. The new word will complete the sentence sensibly.

B 22

Example The cat sprang onto the MO. USE

11 She was DISTRED by the constant noise and found it hard to study. ______

12 That's a BRIANT idea! ______

13 I've THN my old shoes away. ______

14 Why aren't you ALLD to come over? ______

15 Let's grab a bite to eat BEE the film. ______

5

Which one letter can be added to the front of all of these words to make new words?

B 12

Example care cat crate call

16 __ife __ight __ice __oad __urk

17 __ast __ine __ume __ield __ilm

18 __ave __ear __ush __ort __aste

19 __all __and __unch __ook __elm

20 __able __ast __oast __old __ube

5

Move one letter from the first word and add it to the second word to make two new words.

B 13

Example hunt sip hut snip

21 fair deal ______ ______

22 chilly earn ______ ______

23 stage suck ______ ______

24 cover dawn ______ ______

25 feud pond ______ ______

5

Paper 1 (pages 1–5)

1 The **visitors** to the museum stood in the **queue**.
2 **She** had **not** packed any lunch.
3 Most **dogs** like **bones**.
4 I ran upstairs **to get** my book.
5 **He** jumped **out** of the tree.
6 **vanish** 'Appear' means to become visible, so 'vanish', which means to disappear, is the most opposite in meaning.
7 **noisy** 'Silent' means without sound, so 'noisy', which means loud, is the most opposite in meaning.
8 **descend** 'Rise' means to go up, so 'descend', which means to go down, is the most opposite in meaning.
9 **fancy** 'Plain' means lacking in decoration or adornment, so 'fancy', which means highly decorated, is the most opposite in meaning.
10 **solid** 'Runny' means in a liquid state, so 'solid', which means of definite shape and not liquid or gaseous, is the most opposite in meaning.
11–15 Category A contains words to do with animals **(cheetah, weasel)**
Category B contains words to do with fruit **(kiwi, satsuma)**
Category C contains words to do with sport **(rounders, lacrosse, badminton)**
Category D contains words to do with fish **(trout, plaice, salmon)**
16–20 To complete this type of question, try the first word from the first set of brackets with each word in the second set of brackets. Repeat this method with the second and third words from the first set of brackets, until you find the correct combination. It also helps to write the word combinations down for this type of question.
16 **anteater**
17 **laptop**
18 **needless**
19 **friendship**
20 **broadcast**
21 **guess, suspect** Both words mean to 'speculate'.
22 **option, choice** Both words mean to 'have the ability to choose'.
23 **diminish, lessen** Both words mean to 'reduce' or 'decrease'.
24 **ruler, controller** Both words describe someone who is in charge of others.
25 **job, task** Both words mean a 'project' or 'chore'.
26 **Tennis** is the most popular sport. A table is the easiest way to sort the information, like this:

	Tennis	Football	Swimming
Aiden	✓		
Beth		✓	✗
Chloe	✓	✓	✗
Daxa	✓		✓

27–29 This is BIDMAS (Brackets, Indices, Division, Multiplication, Addition, Subtraction). Complete the equation in the brackets first, then complete the rest of the sum.
27 **B** $(6 - 4) \times 2 = 2 \times 2$ which is 4
28 **C** $6 + 4 - 5 = 10 - 5$ which is 5
29 **A** $(2 \times 4) \div 4 = 8 \div 4$ which is 2
30–33 Give two marks for each correct crossword.
30–31

A	N	G	E	L
L	■	R	■	A
E	N	A	C	T
R	■	C	■	C
T	E	E	T	H

32–33

C	A	N	O	E
R	■	I	■	A
E	I	G	H	T
S	■	H	■	E
S	A	T	I	N

34 **KL** Each letter in the first pair moves forward by two places in the second pair.
35 **ON** The first letter in the first pair moves forward by two places in the second pair; the second letter moves back by one place.
36 **GK** The first letter in the first pair moves back by three places in the second pair; the second letter moves forward by three places.
37 **CE** Each letter moves forward by one place.
38 **XU** This is a mirror pair, where the letters are an equal distance from the centre of the alphabet (imagine a mirror line between 'M' and 'N'). AD is a mirror pair to ZW, so CF is a mirror pair to XU.
39–43 Place the letters of the word below or above the symbols to make coding and decoding easier:

H	O	M	E	W	R	K
*	^	%	£	!	~	#

39 **% ^ ~ £**
40 **! ^ ~ %**
41 **% £ £ #**
42 **! * £ ~ £**
43 **~ ^ ^ %**

44–49 These types of questions will need to be read more than once, as the information is not always given in the order you need to work it out in. Begin with James, who is the oldest. Next put in Kate (4th oldest – 'older than just two children'), then Omar ('older than Kate, but younger than Laura", so 3rd oldest) and Laura (older than Omar, so 2nd oldest). As Kate is older than two children and Eva is not the youngest, the final two must be Eva (5th oldest) and Jacob (6th / youngest child).

44 **James**
45 **Laura**
46 **Omar**
47 **Kate**
48 **Eva**
49 **Jacob**

50–54 Look at the numbers that are next to one another in the question. They will have been either been added to, subtracted from, multiplied or divided to get to the next number in the sequence. Sometimes there may be two sequences which alternate in a question: the first, third and fifth numbers follow one sequence and the second, fourth and sixth follow another.

50 **14, 18** The sequence is -3, +4, - 3, +4 etc. (16, 13, 17, 14, 18, 15)
51 **24, 48** Each number in the sequence is multiplied by 2 (3, 6, 12, 24, 48, 96)
52 **6, 9** The sequence is +1, +2, +1, +2 etc. (2, 3, 5, 6, 8, 9)
53 **9, 27** The number added increases by 1 each time: +2, +3, +4, +5 etc. (7, 9, 12, 16, 21, 27)
54 **2, 15** There are two sequences which alternate. In the first sequence, starting with 5, the numbers increase by 5 each time (5, 10, 15). In the second sequence, starting with 1, the numbers increase by 1 each time (1, 2, 3).
55 **t** post, trip
56 **m** worm, moan
57 **t** wart, thaw
58 **e** lice, ease
59 **d** herd, damp

60–64 To complete this type of question, write the letters that have not changed into the space provided for the answer. You can then try changing each of the remaining letters to form a new word. For example:
CASE __AS__ LASH
CASH must be the answer as LASE is not a word.

60 **STEP**
61 **LIVE**
62 **DEER**
63 **BAIL**
64 **GRAB**
65 **about** 'Regarding' and 'concerning' can both be replaced by the word 'about' as can 'roughly' and 'nearly'.
66 **open** 'Unlocked' and 'unfastened' can both be replaced by the word 'open' as can 'start' and 'launch'.
67 **snap** 'Snap' is another word for 'break' or 'crack' and can describe an attack by an animal..
68 **faint** 'Faint' can mean the same as 'faded' and 'dim', but can also be used as a verb meaning to 'collapse' or 'black out'.
69 **cross** Someone who is 'annoyed' or 'grumpy' can be said to be 'cross', whilst a 'cross' is also a shape, as are 'circles' and 'squares'.
70 **Chairs can be made of wood.** For this question you can only judge what must be true based on the given information. Only 'Chairs can be made of wood' must be true as chairs are furniture, which is made out of wood.

71–75 For this type of question it helps to place your fingers over most of the letters, so that only four letters can be seen. Carefully work along the sentence in this way to find the hidden four-letter word. It is worth noting that the pronunciation of some letters might change.

71 **wand** If you blo<u>w and</u> blow the candle will go out.
72 **hear** T<u>he ar</u>gument began when Laurie took Jenna's phone.
73 **chop** Ea<u>ch op</u>ponent must weigh in first.
74 **done** Will you help me fin<u>d one</u> that isn't broken?
75 **test** The rabbits stayed qui<u>te st</u>ill as we passed.
76 **notice** There is no 'c' in 'digestion'.
77 **nineteen** There are only two 'e's in 'intensive'.
78 **dated** There is only one 'd' in 'underneath'.
79 **hurry** There is only one 'r' in 'Thursday'.
80 **drawer** There is only one 'r' in 'answered'.

Paper 2 (pages 5–9)

1–5 Refer to Paper 1 Q50–54 on how to complete this type of question.

1 **56, 28** Each number in the sequence decreases by 7 (63, 56, 49, 42, 35, 28)
2 **16, 128** Each number in the sequence is multiplied by 2 (4, 8, 16, 32, 64, 128)
3 **17, 13** Each number in the sequence decreases by 2 (19, 17, 15, 13, 11, 9)
4 **17, 24** The sequence is +2, +3, +2, +3 etc. (12, 14, 17, 19, 22, 24)

5 **20, 16** The sequence is -3, -1, -3, -1 etc. (27, 24, 23, 20, 19, 16)

6 **17** Emma is 11. Last year she was 10. In 3 years' time Sarah will be 20 (2 × 10) so she is now 17 (20 – 3).

7–11 WALL must be 3255 as this is the only word with double letters. This means W = 3, A = 2, L = 5. LAMP must be 5274 as this is the only code to begin with 5. This means M = 7 and P = 4. E = 6. This means

W	A	L	M	P	E
3	2	5	7	4	6

7 **3255** is WALL

8 **5274** is LAMP

9 **7256** is MALE

10 **4256** is PALE

11 **5624** is LEAP

12 **foal, calf** A 'foal' is a young 'horse' as a 'calf' is a young 'cow'.

13 **driver, pilot** A 'driver' drives a 'car' as a 'pilot' flies an 'aeroplane'.

14 **hasten, gather** 'Hurry' means the same as 'hasten' as 'assemble' means the same as 'gather'.

15 **game, boss** A 'match' can mean a 'game' as a 'head' can mean a 'boss'.

16 **jump, walk** To 'spring' means to 'jump' as to 'march' means to 'walk' (in a particular way).

17 **CROSS**

18 **HOLIDAY**

19 **RULER**

20 **WRIST**

21 **PARTY**

22 **tip** A 'tip' is an 'end' or 'point' and can also mean to 'empty' or 'pour out'.

23 **skip** 'Skip' is a type of movement, as are 'bounce' and 'leap'. It can also mean to 'leave out' or 'miss'.

24 **show** To 'show' can mean to 'guide' or 'teach' and also a 'performance' or 'act'.

25 **place** A 'place' is a 'location' or 'area' and can also mean to 'arrange' or 'put'.

26 **file** A 'file' can be a 'document' or 'folder' and can also mean to 'note' or 'store'.

27–31 Look at the two complete groups of numbers in each question to find if the numbers need to be added to, subtracted from, multiplied or divided. Sometimes there may be two steps needed to complete the equation.

27 **16** Add the two numbers outside the brackets: 3 + 13 = 16

28 **4** Subtract the right-hand number from the left-hand number: 12 – 8 = 4

29 **40** Multiply the numbers outside the brackets: 8 × 5 = 40

30 **15** Add the two numbers outside the brackets, then add 1: 12 + 2 + 1 = 15

31 **25** Add the two numbers outside the brackets: 8 + 17 = 25

32–36 Try each of the words in the first set of brackets. Do they make sense with any words in the second and third set of brackets? Only one combination of three words makes sense.

32 **girl, mother, sweets**

33 **check, work, teacher**

34 **riding, horses, field**

35 **butter, sugar, eggs**

36 **sunny, hot, beach**

37–41 Refer to Paper 1 Q16–20 on how to complete this type of question.

37 **crossroads**

38 **capsize**

39 **useless**

40 **seaweed**

41 **nearby**

42 **c** limb, crack

43 **y** fort, party

44 **s** play, crumbs

45 **i** run, ideal

46 **h** trust, shore

47–51 To complete this type of question, try the first word from the first set of brackets with each word in the second set of brackets. Repeat this method with the second and third words from the first set of brackets, until you find the correct combination.

47 **calm, still** Both words (as adjectives) can mean motionless.

48 **beam, shine** Both words (as verbs) can mean to radiate light.

49 **scratch, graze** Both words (as verbs) can mean to scrape.

50 **fair, honest** Both words (as adjectives) can mean showing integrity and not being deceptive or fraudulent.

51 **force, power** Both words (as nouns) can mean a level of strength or energy.

52 **d** noted, deaf

53 **s** jumps, shape

54 **d** raid, daft

55 **w** knew, wide

56 **g** frog, glee

57 **HIP** CHIPS

58 **ICE** NOTICE

59 **HOP** SHOPPING

60 **EAR** LEARN

61 **TOP** STOPPED

62–65 Give two marks for each correct crossword.

62–63

A	L	O	F	T
G	■	U	■	R
R	I	N	S	E
E	■	C	■	A
E	X	E	R	T

64–65

S	O	C	K	S
T	■	H	■	A
A	C	O	R	N
M	■	I	■	D
P	A	R	T	Y

66 **YB, VE** The first letter in each pair moves back by one place; the second moves forward by one place.
67 **KI, MK** Both letters in each pair move forward by two places.
68 **ZEN, AFO** In this code treat the alphabet as a loop, e.g. W X Y Z A B C etc. Each letter moves forward by one place.
69 **GP, ML** The first letter in each pair moves forward by three letters; the second moves back by two places.
70 **TE, FU** For this sequence look at alternate pairs. Each letter in each alternate pair moves forward by two places (PA, RC, TE and BQ, DS, FU).
71–75 Follow the rules of BIDMAS by completing the equations in the brackets first.
71 **S** $6 + 4 + 2 = 12$
72 **S** $(4 \times 4) - (6 - 2) = 16 - 4 = 12$
73 **T** $4 \times 2 = 8$
74 **P** $12 \div 2 = 6$
75 **Q** $(2 \times 8) \div 4 = 16 \div 4 = 4$
76 **b** bowl, bone, break, bray, brain
77 **j** jam, joint, jump, just, jewel
78 **f** front, foil, flower, force, fool
79 **w** wake, wait, weed, wild, what
80 **n** near, name, neigh, nest, nose

Paper 3 (pages 9–13)

1–5 Category A contains words to do with trees **(pine, willow, oak)**
Category B contains words to do with food **(broccoli, beans, noodles)**
Category C contains words to do with birds **(parrot, eagle, wren, robin)**
6 **clever, dull** The other three words are synonyms meaning 'concept' or 'belief'..
7 **divide, subtract** The other three words are concerned with linking items or people.
8 **nearby, neighbouring** The other three words are adjectives describing something faraway.
9 **lively, sad** The other three words are concerned with the application of power.
10 **lie, complaint** The other three words are concerned with suggestion.
11 **s** moss, salt
12 **p** jump, plum
13 **d** glad, deck
14 **o** solo, onion
15 **k** wink, knit
16–20 Refer to Paper 2 Questions 32–36 on how to answer this type of question.
16 **food, healthy, body**
17 **giraffe, leaves, highest**
18 **stand, tree**
19 **midnight, rainy, night**
20 **asked, mother, computer**
21 **guilty, innocent** 'Guilty' is most opposite to 'innocent' because 'guilty' means responsible for an act whereas 'innocent' means not responsible.
22 **slow, swift** 'Slow' is the most opposite to 'swift' because 'slow' means not fast whereas 'swift' means fast.
23 **joy, sorrow** 'Joy' is the most opposite to 'sorrow' because 'joy' means happiness whereas 'sorrow' means unhappiness.
24 **hazard, safety** 'Hazard' is the most opposite to 'safety' because a 'hazard' is a threat to safety whereas 'safety' is freedom from danger.
25 **accurate, wrong** 'Accurate' is the most opposite to 'wrong' because 'accurate' means correct whereas 'wrong' means incorrect.
26 **daughter** 'Mother' and 'father' are parents in the same way as 'daughter' and 'son' are offspring.
27 **twelve** A 'century' is a period of a hundred years, so refers to the number 'hundred', as 'dozen' refers to 'twelve'.
28 **mine** The word 'mind' becomes 'mine' by changing the last letter from 'd' to 'e' in the same way as 'find' becomes 'fine'.
29 **herd** 'Flock' is a collective noun for 'sheep' in the same way as 'herd' is a collective noun for 'cows'.
30 **Monday** 'January' is preceded by 'December' in the same way as 'Tuesday' is preceded by 'Monday'.
31 **life** lifeboat, lifebuoy, lifeguard, lifejacket
32 **stop** stopgap, stopover, stopwatch, stoppage
33 **fire** fireguard, firefighter, firefly, firepower
34 **wood** woodwork, woodland, woodpecker, woodworm

35 **back** backache, backstroke, backward, backdate
36 **freeze** 'Ice', 'chill' and 'freeze' are all words associated with extreme cold; 'freeze' can also mean to 'stop' or come to a 'standstill'.
37 **side** A 'team' or 'gang' is often referred to as a 'side'; an 'edge' or 'margin' is often called a 'side'.
38 **dull** 'Dull' can mean 'boring' or 'uninteresting'; 'dull' can also mean 'gloomy' or 'cloudy'.
39 **present** 'Present' can mean 'here' or 'attending'; a 'present' is another word for a 'gift' or 'donation'.
40 **track** 'Track' can mean to 'find' or 'hunt'; a 'track' is also a 'path' or 'trail'.
41–43 A table is the easiest way to sort the information, like this:

	Sandwiches	Pear	Apple	Yogurt	Drink	Snack bar
Thomas	✓			✓	✓	
Kasim	✓		✓		✓	✓
Charlotte	✓			✓	✓	
Elena	✓	✓		✓	✗	

41 **2**
42 **Thomas and Charlotte**
43 **Kasim**
44–47 Give two marks for each correct crossword.
44–45

N	■	S	■	A	■
E	X	T	E	N	D
S	■	A	■	G	■
T	I	M	B	E	R
E	■	P	■	R	■
D	I	S	U	S	E

46–47

■	A	■	P	■	M
I	N	S	I	D	E
■	T	■	L	■	S
F	L	O	O	D	S
■	E	■	T	■	E
P	R	I	S	E	D

48–52 Place the letters of the word below or above the symbols to make coding and decoding easier:

<	£	>	/	?	$
S	E	N	I	B	L

48 **SENSE**
49 **LINE**
50 **LESS**
51 **? / > <**
52 **? $ / < <**
53–57 Refer to Paper 1 Questions 50–54 on how to complete this type of question.
53 **25, 33** Each number in the sequence increases by 4 (17, 21, 25, 29, 33, 37)
54 **9, 25** There are two sequences which alternate. In the first sequence, starting with 15, the numbers increase by 5 each time (15, 20, 25). In the second sequence, starting with 9, the numbers increase by 9 each time (9, 18, 27).
55 **6, 3** Each number in the sequence is divided by 2 (96, 48, 24, 12, 6, 3)
56 **44, 32** Each number in the sequence decreases by 3 (47, 44, 41, 38, 35, 32)
57 **44, 69** The number added increases by 1 each time: +9, +10, +11, +12 etc. (14, 23, 33, 44, 56, 69)
58–59 Arrange the words in a grid to make it easier to put them in alphabetical order.

m	o	b	i	l	e	
m	o	d	e	l		
m	o	d	e	m		
m	o	d	e	r	n	
m	o	n	s	t	e	r
m	o	u	l	d		

58 **model**
59 **mould**
60 **mobile**
61–65 Refer to Paper 1 Questions 71–75 on how to answer this type of question.
61 **hold** Sometimes I wash old golf balls then resell them.
62 **nest** Some of the buses went on but mine stopped at the corner.
63 **wear** We are going to paint your room this weekend.
64 **them** The missing cat eventually came home.
65 **neat** Everyone at my office begins at nine.
66–67 **TREE, BOTTOM**
68 **RAIN**
69–70 **LIGHT, NINE**
71 **preen** There is only one 'e' in DESCRIPTION.
72 **dream** There is no 'm' in BREAKDOWN.
73 **grass** There is only one 's' in PLASTERING.
74 **nasty** There is no 'y' in BANNISTER.
75 **honest** There is no 'n' in SILHOUETTE.
76 **ANT** PLANTS
77 **TEN** SENTENCES

78 **OUT** MOUTH
79 **BAT** BATTERY
80 **PEN** SHARPEN

Paper 4 (pages 13–18)

1–5 Refer to Paper 1 Questions 16–20 on how to complete this type of question.
1 **cardboard**
2 **myself**
3 **nothing**
4 **buttercup**
5 **rugby**
6 **PIERCE**
7 **FINE**
8 **ONCE**
9 **LOOSE**
10 **MEAN**
11 **spade** 'Spade' is a card suit, as is a 'club' and 'diamond'; a 'spade' is also a garden tool, as are 'hoes' and 'rakes'.
12 **ring** A 'ring' is an item of jewellery, as is a 'bracelet' and 'necklace'; to give someone a 'ring' can also mean to 'telephone' someone or give them a 'bell'.
13 **cast** 'Cast' means to 'toss' or 'throw'; 'cast' is also a word for a group of 'actors' or 'players'.
14 **comfortable** 'Comfortable' means 'cosy' or 'at ease'; 'comfortable' can also mean 'well-off' or 'wealthy'.
15 **discount** To 'discount' can mean to 'decrease' or 'reduce'; 'discount' can also mean to disregard something, as in 'ignore' or consider 'unimportant'.
16 **trainer, sock** The other three words are all concerned with ways of moving.
17 **hot, spicy** The other three words are all ways of cooking using heat.
18 **idea, drawing** The other three words all mean to make ready before a specific event.
19 **cat, goat** The other three words are all the young of animals or birds.
20 **brown, grass** The other three words are all types of fruit.
21–23 A table is the easiest way to sort the information, like this:

	Departure	Time taken	Arrival
Alice	7.15	1h 30m	8.45
Grace	7.30	45m (half of 1h 30m)	8.15
Lucy	7.45	20m	8.05

21 **8.45 am**
22 **8.15 am**
23 **8.05 am**

24–28 Refer to Paper 1 Questions 50–54 on how to complete this type of question.
24 **19, 21** Each number in the sequence increases by 2 (17, 19, 21, 23, 25, 27)
25 **22, 16** There are two sequences which alternate. In the first sequence, starting with 11, the numbers increase by 11 each time (11, 22, 33). In the second sequence, starting with 14, the numbers increase by 2 each time (14, 16, 18).
26 **3, 18** The sequence is +1, +2, +3, +4 etc. (3, 4, 6, 9, 13, 18)
27 **27, 29** The sequence is +3, +2, +3, +2 etc. (19, 22, 24, 27, 29, 32)
28 **2, 10** There are two sequences which alternate. The first sequence increases by 1 each time (2, 3, 4). The second sequence is increases by 5 each time (5, 10, 15).
29 **ILL** FILLED
30 **HAD** SHADE
31 **AND** SANDY
32 **DEN** SUDDENLY
33 **ELF** SHELF
34 **true, false** 'True' is most opposite to 'false' because 'true' means consistent with fact whereas 'false' means inconsistent with fact.
35 **rear, front** 'Rear' is most opposite to 'front' because 'rear' means the point furthest from the front, whereas 'front' means the point furthest from the rear.
36 **cheeky, polite** 'Cheeky' is the most opposite to 'polite' because 'cheeky' means impertinent and showing poor manners whereas 'polite' means showing good manners.
37 **allow, deny** 'Allow' is the most opposite to 'deny' because 'allow' means to give permission whereas 'deny' means to refuse permission.
38 **total, partial** 'Total' is the most opposite to 'partial' because 'total' means the entirety whereas 'partial' means just a part, rather than the entirety.
39 **k** luck, kiss
40 **b** bulb, bell
41 **w** grow, wasp
42 **k** folk, kerb
43 **t** oat, trace
44–46 For this type of question you can only judge what must be true based on the given information. Some options may be true, but the answer must refer to the statements given.
44 **Goldfish breathe underwater.** From the two statements given, it must be true that 'Goldfish breathe underwater' as goldfish are fish and fish breathe underwater.

45 **Bees make sweet honey.** From the two statements given, it must be true that 'Bees make sweet honey' as bees make honey and honey tastes sweet.

46 **Leather shoes are waterproof.** From the two statements given, it must be true that 'Leather shoes are waterproof' as some shoes are made from leather and leather is waterproof.

47–50 Give two marks for each correct crossword.

47–48

C		T		B	
H	O	R	D	E	S
E		Y		T	
E	X	I	S	T	S
K		N		E	
Y	O	G	U	R	T

49–50

G		S		R	
L	I	T	T	E	R
I		R		C	
D	R	A	W	E	R
E		I		D	
S	U	N	S	E	T

51 **IS** Each letter in the first pair moves forward by one place in the following pair.

52 **OU** The first letter in the first pair moves forward by two places in the following pair; the second letter moves back by two places.

53 **QMT** The first and third letters in the first set move forward by one place in the following set; the second letter moves back by one place.

54 **UW** Each letter in the first pair moves forward by three places in the following pair.

55 **SWP** Each letter in the first set moves back by one place in the following set.

56–60 Arrange the words in a grid to make it easier to put them in alphabetical order.

k	n	e	a	d		
k	n	e	e	c	a	p
k	n	e	e	i	n	g
k	n	i	c	k		
k	n	i	g	h	t	

56 **kneeing**

57 **knick**

58 **knight**

59 **knead**

60 **kneecap**

61–65 Place the letters of the word below or above the symbols to make coding and decoding easier:

C	O	M	P	U	T	E	R	S
?	&	$	*	!	£	@	>	<

61 **STORE**

62 **MOST**

63 **COURSE**

64 **£@>$**

65 **?!£@**

66 **NAME, MEAN**

67 **SNAP, PANS**

68 **MILES, SLIME**

69 **MARCH, CHARM**

70 **SHAPE, PHASE**

71 Dad drives **us to** school in the car.

72 She had **cut** her **knee** badly.

73 I have to **sit** and **wait**.

74 Mum knows we **were** planning to **trick** her.

75 We **went** to the bank to get some **cash**.

76 **22** 5 + 2 + 3 + 6 + 2 + 4

77 **12** 5 + 2 + 1 + 4

78 **20** 6 + 5 + 2 + 1 + 6

79 **21** 3 + 6 + 1 + 5 + 2 + 4

80 **13** 4 + 2 + 2 + 5

Paper 5 (pages 18–22)

1 **doze**

2 **tied**

3 **spot**

4 **bond**

5 **peasant**

6–10 Refer to Paper 2 Questions 47–51 on completing this type of question.

6 **hit, success** Both words are synonyms of' accomplishment' or 'triumph'.

7 **complication, problem** Both words mean a situation that 'frustrates' or 'causes difficulty'.

8 **price, fee** Both words mean the 'cost' for an item or service provided.

9 **imagine, suppose** Both words are synonyms of 'assume' or 'believe to be'.

10 **proof, evidence** Both words mean a 'fact' or 'set of facts, helpful in forming a conclusion or judgement'.

11–15 Refer to Paper 2 Questions 27-31 on how to complete this type of question.

11 **38** Multiply the two numbers outside the brackets and add 2: 12 × 3 = 36, 36 + 2 = 38

12 **2** Divide the left-hand number by the right-hand number: 24 ÷ 12 = 2

13 **24** Add the numbers outside the brackets, then add 5: 7 + 12 = 19, 19 + 5 = 24

14 **5** Subtract the right-hand number from the left-hand number, then subtract 1: 10 – 4 = 6, 6 – 1 = 5

15 **21** Multiply the numbers outside the brackets: 7 × 3 = 21

16 **l** trial, lead; real, light

17 **y** play, yes; try, yellow

18 **g** bring, ghost; rang, grim

19 **b** bulb, black; crib, bald

20 **t** foot, temper; salt, thank

21 **drill** 'Drill' means to 'practise' or 'rehearse'; it can also mean to 'dig' or 'pierce', as in drilling for oil, drilling a hole.

22 **paddle** 'Paddle' is another word for an 'oar' or 'pole'; it can also mean to 'dabble' or 'splash'.

23 **check** 'Check' means to 'review' or 'inspect'; it can also mean to 'stop' or 'limit'.

24 **boom** 'Boom' can refer to the 'sound made when something explodes or roars'; it can also be used to mean 'success or growth', particularly in business.

25 **force** 'Force' can mean 'strength' or 'energy'; it can also mean to 'make' or 'cause' someone to act in a particular way.

26 **photo** There is only one 'o' in TELEPHONES.

27 **sauce** There is no 'c' in STATUES.

28 **feast** There is no 'a' in PETRIFIES.

29 **start** There is only one 't' in CHRISTMAS.

30 **drains** There is no 'n' in RADISHES.

31 **clap**

32 **plain**

33 **feast**

34 **hire**

35 **yearn**

36–40 Refer to Paper 1 Questions 71–75 on how to answer this type of question.

36 **slat** The clock struck twelve and minute**s lat**er we left.

37 **stem** The be**st em**eralds are used for jewellery.

38 **side** Some of hi**s ide**as were a bit unusual.

39 **toad** Some people find it hard **to ad**mit when they are wrong.

40 **noon** We made sure that **no on**e missed their turn.

41–45 Refer to Paper 1 Questions 60–64 on how to answer this type of question.

41 **WILD**

42 **WITH**

43 **HALT**

44 **OVEN**

45 **BIND**

46 **still** 'Still' means the same as 'calm', just as 'nimble' means the same as 'agile'.

47 **dislike** 'Dislike' and 'enjoy' are antonyms, as are 'soothe' (which means to calm) and 'disturb' (which means to break up the state of calm).

48 **sparse** 'Sparse' is an antonym of 'numerous', as 'grim' is an antonym of 'pleasant'.

49 **welcome** 'Welcome' is a synonym of 'greet,' just as 'pleased' is a synonym of 'delighted'.

50 **rise** 'Rise' is an antonym of 'descend', just as 'seldom' is an antonym of 'often'.

51–56 Give two marks for each correct crossword.

51–52

	A		T		A
P	R	E	E	N	S
	R		M		P
S	I	M	P	L	E
	V		L		C
C	E	M	E	N	T

53–54

	B		R		S
R	E	V	E	R	T
	H		V		Y
R	E	V	E	A	L
	L		R		E
A	D	D	E	R	S

55–56

	O		F		L
A	C	T	I	V	E
	T		N		A
N	A	T	I	O	N
	V		S		E
T	E	T	H	E	R

57–60 Refer to Paper 1 Questions 50–54 on how to complete this type of question.

57 **29, 43** The sequence is +4, +5, + 4, +5 etc. (16, 20, 25, 29, 34, 38, 43)

58 **72, 48** The number decreases by 8 each time (72, 64, 56, 48, 40, 32, 24)

59 **72, 45** The number subtracted decreases by 2 each time: -13, -11, -9, -7 etc. (85, 72, 61, 52, 45, 40, 37)

60 **10, 24** There are two sequences which alternate. In the first sequence, starting with 6, the numbers increase by 6 each time (6, 12, 18, 24). In the second sequence the numbers increase by 10 each time (10, 20, 30).

61–65 The easiest way to complete this type of question is to put the example given in a grid and write how many places the letter has been moved along the alphabet. Then complete another grid and use the same rule to find out the code or letters in the answer:

T	H	I	R	D
+2	+2	+2	+2	+2
V	J	K	T	F

61 **NJDF** To get from the word to the code, move each letter forwards by one place.
62 **LWOR** To get from the word to the code, move each letter forwards by two places.
63 **KHMD** In this code treat the alphabet as a loop, e.g. W X Y Z A B C etc. To get from the word to the code, move each letter backwards by one place.
64 **PURSE** To get from the code to the word, move each letter in the code forwards by two places.
65 **YOUNG** To get from the code to the word, move each letter in the code backwards by one place.
66–71 Follow the rules of BIDMAS by completing any equations in brackets first.
66 **D** $4 + 8 - 2 = 10$
67 **C** $10 \times 2 = 20$, $20 \div 4 = 5$
68 **A** $(8 + 4) - 10 = 12 - 10 = 2$
69 **D** $5 \times 2 = 10$
70 **E** $(10 - 4) + (8 \div 4) = 6 + 2 = 8$
71 **B** $(4 \times 2) - (2 \times 2) = 8 - 4 = 4$
72 **10** Tom's dog is now 6. His hamster is therefore 3. His cat is $3 + 7 = 10$.
73 **ADELOPT**
74 **M** In alphabetical order MOVED is DEMOV. The letter 'M' is then in the middle.
75 **December** In alphabetical order the months of the year are April, August, December etc, making December the third month.
75–80 Arrange the words in grids to make it easier to put them in the correct alphabetical order.
76 **2 3 4 1**

r	e	t	h	g	u	a	d
t	h	g	u	a	t		
t	h	g	u	o	h	t	
y	t	h	g	u	a	n	

77 **4 3 1 2**

e	c	i	u	j			
e	c	n	a	s	i	u	n
t	i	u	r	f			
t	i	u	s				

78 **2 1 3 4**

s	u	o	i	x	n	a	
s	u	o	l	u	b	a	f
s	u	o	m	a	f		
s	u	o	m	r	o	n	e

79 **3 1 4 2**

s	s	e	n	i	p	p	a	h	
s	s	e	n	i	s	m	u	l	c
s	s	e	n	l	l	i			
s	s	e	n	t	i	f			

80 **1 4 2 3**

e	l	b	i	r	r	e	t
e	l	b	i	r	r	o	h
l	e	e	h	w			
l	e	r	r	i	u	q	s

Paper 6 (pages 23–27)

1 **KJ, ED** Each letter moves back two places in the next pair.
2 **KR, VW** The first letter in each pair moves forward by one extra place each time, i.e. one place forward, then two places, then three, then four. The second letter in each pair moves forward by one place less each time, i.e. six places forward, then five, then four, then three, etc.
3 **CX, GT** The first letter in each pair moves forward by two places. The second letter moves back by two places.
4 **IN, FQ** The first letter in each pair moves back by one place. The second letter in each pair moves forward by one place.
5 **VU, EF** There are two sequences which alternate. Pairs one, three and five begin at the end of the alphabet and move backwards through the letters: ZY XW VU. Pairs two, four and six begin at the beginning of the alphabet and move forwards through the letters: AB CD EF.
6–11 Give two marks for each correct crossword.

6–7

	T		T		G
B	E	A	R	E	R
	L		I		A
E	L	O	P	E	D
	E		L		E
F	R	I	E	N	D

8–9

B		U		I	
A	S	S	U	M	E
N		H		M	
A	V	E	N	U	E
N		R		N	
A	N	S	W	E	R

10–11

A		S		B	
N	E	E	D	E	D
G		A		C	
L	E	S	S	O	N
E		O		M	
S	U	N	S	E	T

12 **le** nettle, leopard
13 **st** roast, sting
14 **er** former, errand
15 **be** globe, beware
16 **on** option, onion
17–21 Refer to Paper 2 Questions 32–36 on how to answer this type of question.
17 **turn, ride, bike**
18 **picked, strawberries, field**
19 **dry, plates, cupboard**
20 **goggles, swim**
21 **complain, loud, music**
22–24 Refer to Paper 1 Questions 71–75 on how to answer this type of question.
22 **head** Amy immediately posted her cards as s**he ad**dressed them.
23 **meat** William, please co**me at** once.
24 **them** The sunset bathed **the m**ountain in golden light.
25 **abundant, plentiful** Both words describe 'great quantities'.
26 **answer, reply** Both words mean to 'respond'.
27 **rhythm, beat** Both words describe 'tempo' or 'pulse'.
28 **alter, change** Both words mean to 'adjust' or 'make something different'.
29 **injury, damage** Both words describe a type of 'wound' or 'hurt'.
30 **Raj** A table is the easiest way to sort the information, like this:

	Country	Town	Cinema	Drama club
Hannah	✓			
Charlie	✓		✓	
Raj		✓	✓	✓
Daisy		✓		✓

31–33 A table is the easiest way to see the code, like this:

P	R	E	V	I	O	U	S
7	9	6	4	3	5	8	2

31 **SURE**
32 **PURSE**
33 **ROPE**
34 **UVYW**

P	R	E	T	E	N	D
T	U	V	W	X	Y	Z

This shows that RENT = UVYW.
35 **HEAD**

S	H	A	D	E
2	4	5	3	6

This shows that 4653 = HEAD
36–40 Follow the rules of BIDMAS by completing any equations in brackets first.
36 **9** $6 + 2 + 1 = 9$
37 **28** $(5 \times 2) + (3 \times 6) = 10 + 18 = 28$
38 **4** $(3 + 6) - (1 \times 5) = 9 - 5 = 4$
39 **1** $(3 \times 2) \div (1 \times 6) = 6 \div 6 = 1$
40 **24** There is one D (4), two R ($2 \times 5 = 10$), two E ($2 \times 2 = 4$), two S ($2 \times 3 = 6$) $4 + 10 + 4 + 6 = 24$
41 **ARE** PARENTS
42–43 **THE** CLOTHES, **LIP** SLIPPERS
44–45 **RAP** GRAPES, **PEN** RIPENED
46 **assortment** 'Assortment' means a group of varied items, which is closest in meaning to 'collection', which means a group of objects kept together.
47 **instructor** 'Instructor' and 'coach' both mean a person who trains or teaches others.
48 **outside** 'Outside' and 'exterior' mean outdoors.
49 **fixed** 'Fixed' and 'stable' both mean unmoving.
50 **blend** 'Blend' and 'mix' both mean to combine, as with ingredients in a recipe.
51–55 To complete this type of question, write the letter that has not changed into the spaces provided for the answers: TEAK __E___ __E___ RENT. Then try changing each of

the remaining letters, one at a time, into the letters shown in the final word. The first word could be one of the following: REAK, TENK or TEAT. TEAT is the only one that is a real word, so this is the first answer. This means that the following word will be __E__T, so the second word could be REAT or TENT. REAT is not a real word, so the answer is TENT.

51 **PALM, PALE**
52 **HARK, HARE**
53 **WART, WARS**
54 **BITE, BILE**
55 **DAZE, MAZE**
56 <u>cap</u>, **helmet** You should always wear a safety helmet when riding a bicycle.
57 <u>garden</u>, **garage** She put her car in the garage every night.
58 <u>trying</u>, **writing** Copy the poem again; your writing isn't neat enough.
59 <u>moon</u>, **sun** The sun was shining by midday, so he ate his lunch in the garden.
60 <u>winter</u>, **summer** We sit in the garden until dark during the long days of summer.
61 **r** though, frog
62 **o** bat, mouse
63 **t** ray, them
64 **l** bend, black
65 **e** chat, least
66 **out** outskirts, outside, outline, outburst
67 **up** upon, update, uproar, upset
68 **under** undergo, undertake, underline, undergrowth
69 **tea** teaspoon, teacake, teatime, teacup
70 **post** postbox, postcard, postcode, postage
71 **bead**
72 **fade**
73 **decade**
74 **café**
75 **face**
76–79 Category A contains words to do with clothing **(linen, waistcoat).**
Category B contains words to do with the coast **(sand, diving, cliffs).**
Category C contains words to do with the calendar **(era, annual, Monday)**
80 **Some animals live in rainforests.** For this question you can only judge what is true based on the information given. As a monkey is an animal and some monkeys live in the rainforests it must be true that 'some animals live in rainforests'. There is no evidence in the sentences that <u>most</u> monkeys live in rainforests or that rainforests are hot places. It is not <u>stated</u> that monkeys climb trees.

Paper 7 (pages 27–31)

1–5 Arrange the words in a grid to make it easier to put them in alphabetical order.

P	R	O	S	P	E	C	T	
P	R	O	S	P	E	R		
P	R	O	V	I	N	C	E	
P	R	O	V	I	S	I	O	N
P	R	O	V	O	K	E		

1 **PROSPECT**
2 **PROVOKE**
3 **PROVINCE**
4 **PROVISION**
5 **PROSPER**
6 **crisp** 'Stale', which means 'old' and 'beginning to deteriorate', is the most opposite of 'crisp', which can mean 'fresh' and 'new'.
7 **listener** 'Speaker', which means 'someone who is speaking', is the most opposite of 'listener', which can mean 'someone who is listening to a speaker'.
8 **idle** 'Busy', which means 'engaged in activity', is the most opposite of 'idle' which means 'inactive'.
9 **shorten** 'Extend', which means to 'make longer', is the most opposite of 'shorten', which means to 'make shorter'.
10 **connect** 'Break', which can mean to 'separate' or 'fracture', is the most opposite of 'connect', which means to 'join together'.
11 **ACT** DISTR<u>**ACT**</u>ED
12 **ILL** BR<u>**ILL**</u>IANT
13 **ROW** TH<u>**ROW**</u>N
14 **OWE** ALL<u>**OWE**</u>D
15 **FOR** BE<u>**FOR**</u>E
16 **l** life, light, lice, load, lurk
17 **f** fast, fine, fume, field, film
18 **p** pave, pear, push, port, paste
19 **h** hall, hand, hunch, hook, helm
20 **c** cable, cast, coast, cold, cube
21 **i** far, ideal
22 **y** chill, yearn
23 **t** sage, stuck
24 **r** cove, drawn
25 **u** fed, pound

26–30 The code is made by moving each letter forward by one place in the alphabet and changing from capital letters to lower case ones. It might be helpful to draw a chart:

A	B	C	D	E	F	G	H	I	J	K	L	M
b	c	d	e	f	g	h	i	j	k	l	m	n
N	O	P	Q	R	S	T	U	V	W	X	Y	Z
o	p	q	r	s	t	u	v	w	x	y	z	a

Place each of the codes or words in a table, as shown, to help work out the answers:

26 **gpsl**
27 **tqppo**
28 **dvq**
29 **KNIFE**
30 **SAUCER**
31 **B** It may be helpful to draw a diagram to help with relative positions:

	C	
D	A	
		B

32–36 Start with POUCH as this is the only five-letter word. From this we know that POUCH = 64782. That tells you that P = 6, O = 4, U = 7, C = 8 and H = 2. Next is HOPS which is the only other word containing the letter 'O'. HOPS is 2465, so S = 5. PUSH must therefore be 6752 and CHAP = 8236. CHOPS can now be worked out.

P	O	U	C	H	S	A
6	4	7	8	2	5	3

32 **6752** is PUSH
33 **2465** is HOPS
34 **8236** is CHAP
35 **64782** is POUCH
36 **82465** is CHOPS
37 **courage, bravery** Both words mean to show 'fearlessness' and 'daring'.
38 **glance, look** Both words mean to 'catch sight of'.
39 **halt, stop** Both words mean to 'come to a standstill'.
40 **cross, angry** Both words mean to be 'infuriated'.
41 **tint, colour** Both words mean 'tone' or 'hue'.
42 **brief, amazing** 'Brief' means the same as 'short', just as 'incredible' means the same as 'amazing'.
43 **fruit, vegetable** A pear is a fruit just as a cabbage is a vegetable.
44 **listening, tasting** An ear is used for listening, just as a mouth is used for tasting.
45 **active, pity** 'Active' has a similar meaning to 'vigorous', just as 'sympathy' has a similar meaning to 'pity'.
46 **fragile, squander** 'Fragile' is the opposite of 'tough', just as 'save' is the opposite of 'squander'.
47 **he** soothe, healthy
48 **on** upon, once
49 **ce** office, cereal
50 **us** circus, usual
51 **in** plain, invent
52 **ROBIN**
53 **CINEMA**
54 **MAGICIAN**
55 **CAMEL**
56 **COMMENCE**

57–61 Refer to Paper 1 Questions 50–54 on how to complete this type of question.

57 **65, 36** There are two sequences which alternate. In the first sequence, starting with 75, the number decreases by 5 each time (75, 70, 65, 60). In the second sequence, starting with 28, the number increases by 4 each time (28, 32, 36).
58 **24, 30** Each number in the sequence increases by 6 (6, 12, 18, 24, 30, 36, 42).
59 **85, 103** In this sequence the number added increases by 2 each time: +2, +4, +6, +8 etc.
60 **125, 50** Each number in the sequence decreases by 25.
61 **12, 16** There are two sequences which alternate. In the first sequence, starting with 6, the number increases by 3 each time (6, 9, 12, 15). In the second sequence, starting with 8, the number increases by 4 each time (8, 12, 16).
62 **SPIN**
63 **PIER**
64 **STAGE**
65 **CHEAT**
66 **TRAP**
67 **day, month** The shortest month of the year is February.
68 **chair, table** I reserved a table for two at the restaurant.
69 **cheap, expensive** Her father complained that the telephone bill was too expensive.
70 **tail, claws** The kitten scratched our new chair with her claws.
71 **tea, water** She boiled just enough water in the kettle to make a hot drink.
72 **In** which year **was** the big storm?
73 It is important that **each form** is filled in completely.

74 **Some** friends **from** Australia are visiting.
75 We picked **up** shells **on** the beach.
76 I **admit** that I have **made** a mistake.
77–80 Give two marks for each correct crossword.

77–78

	P		D		C
L	A	V	I	S	H
	V		S		E
D	E	F	U	S	E
	R		S		R
A	S	S	E	T	S

79–80

	B		B		S
D	O	C	I	L	E
	T		T		A
W	H	I	T	E	R
	E		E		C
D	R	E	N	C	H

Paper 8 (pages 32–36)

1 **tadpole** A caterpillar is the younger stage of a butterfly, as a tadpole' is the younger stage of a 'frog'.
2 **kind** 'Vacant' is the opposite of 'occupied', as 'kind' is the opposite of 'mean'.
3 **keys** A clock has hands, as a piano has keys.
4 **suggest** 'Fair' means the same as 'just', as 'suggest' means the same as 'imply'.
5 **export** 'Fact' is the opposite of 'fiction', as 'import' is the opposite of 'export'.
6 **water** watercress, watercolour, waterfall, watermelon
7 **land** landlady, landmark, landslide, landlord
8 **day** daylight, daybreak, daydream, daytime
9 **rain** raincoat, rainbow, raindrop, rainfall
10 **wind** windfall, windburn, windmill, windbreak
11 **snowdrop** All the words are types of flower.
12 **wail** All the words are concerned with loud voices.
13 **soar** All the words mean to move in an upwards direction.
14 **spring** All the words are names of seasons.
15 **rain** All the words are concerned with types of weather linked with water.
16 **RAT** CELEBRATE
17 **WIN** CHEWING
18 **OUR** COLOURFUL
19 **TEN** ATTEND
20 **EAT** BREATHE
21–24 Give two marks for each correct crossword.

21–22

	H		H		L
S	A	V	A	G	E
	N		L		A
E	D	I	T	E	D
	L		E		E
N	E	A	R	E	R

23–24

	C		R		S
C	R	O	U	C	H
	E		M		I
M	A	R	B	L	E
	K		L		L
A	S	C	E	N	D

25–30 Firstly, 'VASES' must be 25979 as it has the same third and fifth number. Thus V = 2, A = 5, S = 9 and E = 7. 'LEAVE' = 37527 because of the position of the number 7. This means L = 3. RIVAL = 86253 because it has V (2) as third letter. This leaves SLIMY = 93641. This code can best be shown in a table:

A	E	I	L	M	R	S	V	Y
5	7	6	3	4	8	9	2	1

25 **86253** is RIVAL
26 **25979** is VASES
27 **37527** is LEAVE
28 **93641** is SLIMY
29 **RAIL**
30 **REVEAL**
31 **TS, KJ** Both letters in each pair move back by three places.
32 **FR, GS** Both letters in each pair move forward by one place.
33 **MH, KI** The first letter in each pair moves back by two places. The second letter in each pair moves forward by one place.
34 **PT, UY** Both letters in each pair move forward by five places.
35 **KO, QW** The first letter in each pair moves forward by three places. The second letter in each pair moves forward by four places.
36 **bleed** There is no 'd' in BREAKABLE.
37 **tests** There is only one 's' in POTATOES.
38 **overstay** There is no 'a' in CONTROVERSY.
39 **ginger** There is no 'r' in BELONGINGS.
40 **leader** There is only one 'e' in DREADFUL.

41–45 Refer to Paper 2 Questions 32–36 on how to answer this type of question.

41 **burnt, oven**
42 **Tired, sleep, school**
43 **dog, kennel, raining**
44 **question, plan, answer**
45 **pleased, holiday, summer**
46 **k** bark, kettle; walk, know
47 **n** bean, nest; grin, nose
48 **e** face, ease; sale, east
49 **b** rob, bold; comb, black
50 **t** fort, task; wart, tent

51–55 Use grids as shown below to help work out the missing word.

51 **HAVE**

1	2		
B	O	W	L

3	4		
R	E	A	D

1	2		
H	A	R	D

3	4		
V	E	S	T

52 **NOSE**

2			1
H	I	N	T

4		3	
W	E	A	K

2			1
O	P	E	N

4		3	
E	A	S	Y

53 **PALM**

		4	1
T	I	E	D

		2	3	
F	R	O	N	T

		4	1
L	I	M	P

		2	3	
S	T	A	L	E

54 **MOAN**

		3	4
B	A	L	L

1	2			
W	E	I	R	D

		3	4
L	E	A	N

1	2			
M	O	I	S	T

55 **STAR**

4		3		
P	R	A	Y	S

			1	2
P	A	T	C	H

4		3		
R	O	A	S	T

			1	2
W	R	I	S	T

56–58 Arrange the words in a grid to make it easier to put them in the correct alphabetical order.

D	E	S	C	E	N	D	
D	E	S	C	R	I	B	E
D	E	S	E	R	V	E	
D	E	S	I	R	E		
D	E	S	P	A	I	R	

56 **DESIRE**
57 **DESCEND**
58 **DESCRIBE**

59–60 These types of questions will need to be read more than once, as the information is not always given in the order you need to work it out in. A table is the easiest way to sort the information, like this:

	Time taken	Position	
A	7 mins	1st	This is the fourth calculation (9 – 2).
B	11 mins	3rd	This is the final calculation (7 + 4).
C	9 mins	2nd	This is the third calculation (12 – 3).
D	15 mins	5th	Begin calculating with D.
E	12 mins	4th	This is the second calculation (15 – 3).

59 D
60 9

61–64 Follow the rules of BIDMAS by completing any equations in brackets first.

61 **7** $(2 \times 3) + 1 = 6 + 1 = 7$
62 **2** $\frac{6}{3} = 6 \div 3 = 2$
63 **10** $(5 \times 4) \div 2 = 20 \div 2 = 10$
64 **9** $3 \times 3 = 9$
65 **Rings can be made of metal.** For this question you can only judge what is true based on the information given. As 'rings can be made of gold' and 'gold is a metal', the only sentence that must be true is 'Rings can be made of metal'. There is no evidence in the two sentences that other statements must be true. For example, although gold may be an expensive metal it is not stated in the two sentences.
66 **vague, certain** 'Vague' and 'certain' are most opposite because 'vague' means to be 'approximate', whereas 'certain' means 'in no doubt'.
67 **scatter, collect** 'Scatter' and 'collect' are most opposite because 'scatter' means to 'distribute', whereas 'collect' means to 'bring together'.
68 **satisfy, disappoint** 'Satisfy' and 'disappoint' are most opposite because 'satisfy' means to 'meet expectations' whereas 'disappoint' means to 'fail to meet expectations'.
69 **undermine, enhance** 'Undermine' and 'enhance' are most opposite because 'undermine' means to 'reduce effectiveness', often by a form of sabotage, whereas 'enhance' means to 'increase the effectiveness of something'.
70 **unusual, ordinary** 'Unusual' and 'ordinary' are most opposite because 'unusual' means 'uncommon' whereas 'ordinary' means 'common'.

71–75 Refer to Paper 1 Questions 16–20 on how to complete this type of question.

71 **insect**
72 **throughout**
73 **nomad**
74 **attempt**

75 **beam**

76–80 Refer to Paper 5 Questions 61–65 on how to answer this type of question.

76 **AMPYJ** To get from the word to the code, move each letter back by two places.

77 **CNKDK** To get from the word to the code, move each letter forward by two places.

78 **RIGHT** In this code treat the alphabet as a loop, e.g. W X Y Z A B C etc. To get from the code to the word, move each letter forward by four places.

79 **ICUFTAY** To get from the word to the code, move the first letters forward by one place, the second forward by two places, the third forward by three places, the fourth forward by four places, etc.

80 **BQDG** To get from the word to the code, move the first and third letters forward by one place; more the second and fourth letters back by one place.

Paper 9 (pages 36–40)

1 **MENTAL, LAMENT**

2 **STATE, TASTE**

3 **REWARD, DRAWER**

4 **CRATE, REACT**

5 **STOAT, TOAST**

6 **amount** 'Amount' is most similar to 'quantity' as both words refer to a specified number or size.

7 **stroll** 'Stroll' is most similar to 'ramble' as both mean to 'walk' or 'wander'.

8 **difficult** 'Difficult' is most similar to 'awkward' as both can refer to challenging situations.

9 **scrape** 'Scrape' is most similar to 'graze' as both can mean a 'minor scratch on the skin'.

10 **talent** 'Talent' is most similar to 'flair' as both mean a 'particular ability at something'.

11–15 To get from the word to the code, move each letter back by two places. After the letter 'Z' count forward through 'A' to 'B'. To get from the code to the word move each letter forward by two places. A chart might help:

Word:	A	B	C	D	E	F	G	H	I	J	K	L	M
	N	O	P	Q	R	S	T	U	V	W	X	Y	Z
Code:	Y	Z	A	B	C	D	E	F	G	H	I	J	K
	L	M	N	O	P	Q	R	S	T	U	V	W	X

Place each of the codes or words in a table, as shown, to help work out the answers:

B	O	T	T	O	M
−2	−2	−2	−2	−2	−2
Z	M	R	R	M	K

11 **TOMB**

12 **GROUND**

13 **GARDEN**

14 **CYPRF**

15 **JMUCQR**

16–20 Refer to Paper 1 Questions 71–75 on how to answer this type of question.

16 **twin** The team did no<u>t win</u> a single match this year.

17 **form** I hope I can have a brand new phone <u>**for m**</u>y birthday.

18 **peel** I do ho<u>pe el</u>even pounds isn't too much to spend.

19 **heal** <u>She al</u>ways helps out when needed.

20 **sour** Money is al<u>**so ur**</u>gently needed by the charity.

21–27 Refer to Paper 2 Questions 47–51 on completing this type of question.

21 **open, closed** 'Open' means not 'unfastened', so 'closed', which means 'fastened', is the most opposite in meaning.

22 **war, peace** 'War' means a 'state of conflict', so 'peace', which means a 'lack of hostility or war', is the most opposite in meaning.

23 **alert, distracted** 'Alert' means to be 'attentive' and 'mentally responsive', so 'distracted', which means to 'have the attention diverted' and thus not be mentally responsive, is most opposite in meaning.

24 **deliberate, accidental** 'Deliberate' means 'with intent', so 'accidental', which means 'without intent', is most opposite in meaning.

25 **essential, unimportant** 'Essential' means 'vital' or 'important', so 'unimportant', which means 'lacking importance', is most opposite in meaning.

26 **flee, remain** 'Flee' means to 'run away', so 'remain', which means to 'stay', is the most opposite in meaning.

27 **mad, sane** 'Mad' means 'mentally ill', so 'sane', which means 'of sound mind', is the most opposite in meaning.

28–29 For these types of questions you can only judge what is true based on the information given.

28 **Some African mammals may feed on leaves.** Herds are not mentioned in the two sentences, nor is it stated that <u>most</u> of the animals in Africa are mammals. There is also nothing to suggest that many plants are found only in Africa. However, since it is stated that 'Many mammals are plant-eaters' and 'Some mammals live in Africa', it must be true that 'some African mammals may feed on leaves'.

29 **Sounds can be represented by letters.** There is no mention of words usually being written, nor that there are many different languages. It is not stated that 'all languages use the same alphabet' either. However, since it is stated that 'Letters are used for each sound in a word', it follows that 'Sounds can be represented by letters'.

30–35 Give two marks for each correct crossword.

30–31

L	A	P
E	G	O
D	O	T

32–33

T	O	E
W	A	Y
O	R	E

34–35

D	I	P
A	C	E
M	E	T

36–40 Refer to Paper 1 Questions 50–54 on how to complete this type of question.

36 **6, 15** Each number in the sequence increases by 3.

37 **27, 37** The number added increases by 2 each time: +2, +4, +6, +8, etc.

38 **55, 15** The number subtracted decreases by 2 each time: -13, -11, -9, -7, etc.

39 **14, 22** Each number in the sequence increases by 8.

40 **28, 24** There are two sequences which alternate. In the first sequence, starting with 14, the numbers increase by 7 each time (14, 21, 28, 35). In the second sequence, starting with 36, the numbers decrease by 6 each time (36, 30, 24).

41 **in** chain, invade

42 **se** cause, serious

43 **al** normal, always

44 **er** remember, error

45 **st** toast, street

46 **litre, kilogram** The other three words are measurements of length.

47 **look, march** The other three words refer to the volume of oral communication.

48 **clear, weather** The other three words mean uninteresting.

49 **London, France** The other three words are nouns referring to population centres, but not their proper names.

50 **hinder, depress** The other three words refer to advancing and supporting.

51 **rock** 'Rock' is similar to 'stone' and 'pebble' and can also mean to 'sway' or 'wobble'.

52 **snappy** 'Snappy' can mean 'irritable' or 'cross' and can also be used to mean 'brisk' or 'lively' (as in the phrase 'make it snappy').

53 **understanding** An 'understanding' is similar in meaning to an 'idea' or 'knowledge' and also means an 'agreement' or 'pact'.

54 **class** 'Class' can mean a 'division' or 'group' (as in 'type' or 'category'). It can also refer to a standard achieved, as in a 'grade' awarded at the end of a 'course'.

55 **blossom** 'Blossom' is another word for the flowers on trees or bushes, which, in their younger state, are buds. It can also mean to 'grow' and' 'progress'.

56 **site** Add the letter 'e' to the first word.

57 **over** Remove the first letter from the first word.

58 **fate** Change the first letter of the first word from 'd' to 'f'.

59 **sire** Swap the first and third letters.

60 **has** Remove the first letter and move the second and third letters to the end of the word.

61 **FADE**

62 **REAL**

63 **BRIEF**

64 **RAGE**

65 **LAPSE**

66–70 Refer to Paper 2 Questions 32–36 on how to answer this type of question.

66 **go, cinema, week**

67 **autumn, leaves, fall**

68 **friends, play, park**

69 **parents, watching, television**

70 **clock, time, second**

71–75 As AREA begins and ends with 'A', its code must be 5635. This means A = 5, R = 6 and E = 3. As ROPE is the only word to end with 'E', its code must be 6243, meaning P = 4 and O = 2. PEAR must be 4356 and SOAP must be 7254. This means A = 5, R = 6, E = 3, O = 2, P = 4 and S = 7.

A	R	E	P	O	S
5	6	3	4	2	7

71 **4356** is PEAR

72 **5635** is AREA

73 **7254** is SOAP

74 **6243** is ROPE
75 **4273** is POSE
76 **get, stay** As it's Saturday tomorrow, you can stay up late to watch the film.
77 **spent, saved** She saved her pocket money because she couldn't find anything tempting to buy.
78 **hair, teeth** Brush your teeth after eating so many sweets.
79 **songs, movies** or **films** Our cinema doesn't always show the most recent movies / films.
80 **hungry, thirsty** She took a sip of her drink because she was thirsty.

Paper 10 (pages 41–45)

1 **NH, OI** Both letters move forward by one place each time.
2 **KZ, PU** The first letter in each pair moves forward by one extra place each time, i.e. one place forward, then two places, then three, etc. The second letter in each pair moves back by one extra place each time, i.e. one place back, then two places, then three etc. (Treat the alphabet as a loop, e.g. W X Y Z A B C etc.)
3 **ID, FF** The first letter in each pair moves back by one place less each time, i.e. five places back, then four places, then three etc. The second letter repeats, then moves forward two places, then repeats, then moves forward two places, etc. (B, B, D, D, F, F)
4 **FV, CY** The first letter moves back by one place each time; the second letter moves forward by one place each time.
5 **MP, NO** The first letter moves forward one place, then two, then one, then two (+1, +2, +1, +2) etc. The second letter moves back one place, then two, then one, then two (−1, −2, −1, −2) etc.
6 **husband, wife** 'Wife' is the female equivalent of 'husband', just as 'aunt' is the female equivalent of 'uncle'.
7 **unite, join** 'Unite' means the same as 'join', just as 'reveal' means the same as 'show'.
8 **pig, sty** A pig's home is a sty, just as a lion's home is a den.
9 **spirited, vigorous** 'Spirited' can mean the same as 'vigorous', just as 'sad' can mean the same as 'melancholy'.
10 **deny, admit** 'Deny' means the opposite of 'admit', just as 'depart' means the opposite of 'arrive'.
11 **RAN** ARRANGE
12 **ONE** LONELY
13 **EAR** CLEARLY
14 **PEA** REPEATING
15 **ASK** MASKS
16–20 Follow the rules of BIDMAS by completing any equations in brackets first. When letters are placed next to one another, without a +, − × or ÷ sign between them, they need to be multiplied.
16 **21** $6 + 5 + 10 = 21$
17 **4** $(2 \times 10) \div 5 = 20 \div 5 = 4$
18 **17** $(6 \times 2) + 5 = 12 + 5 = 17$
19 **0** $6 \times 2 \times 0 = 0$
20 **5** $(5 \times 10) \div (2 \times 5) = 50 \div 10 = 5$
21 **s** seek, sick, score, self, sack
22 **l** loyal, lure, luck, list, load
23 **h** hook, hoot, horn, hour, host
24 **d** dire, dice, deed, deal, dale
25 **t** toad, tool, tent, tank, tuck
26 **guest** A 'guest' is receiving hospitality, so is most opposite to a 'host' who is providing it.
27 **limited** 'Limited' means restricted, so is most opposite to 'endless' which means 'without restriction or limit'.
28 **drop** 'Drop' means to fail to catch (e.g. a ball), so is most opposite to 'catch'.
29 **approve** 'Approve' means to 'show agreement', so is most opposite to 'object' which means to 'put forward an argument against'.
30 **genuine** 'Genuine' means 'real', so is most opposite to 'artificial' which means 'an imitation'.
31 **STAMP**
32 **PROUD**
33 **INVITED**
34 **ACCIDENT**
35 **PURSE**
36–39 Give two marks for each correct crossword.
36–37

	I		E		S
A	M	I	D	S	T
	P		I		O
M	A	T	T	E	D
	R		O		G
S	T	O	R	E	Y

38–39

	C		S		A
L	O	I	T	E	R
	U		A		C
C	R	U	T	C	H
	S		E		E
C	E	N	S	O	R

40 **Some people drink Chinese tea.** For this question you can only judge what is true based on the information given. In the two sentences there is no evidence that 'most people in China grow tea plants' or that 'tea is a more popular drink than coffee'. It is not stated that tea is a hot drink, even though that may be true. However, 'Tea is grown in China' and 'Many people drink tea' so it must be true that 'Some people drink Chinese tea'.

41–46 TEAM begins with the letter 'T' and EAST ends with it, so TEAM is 1537 and EAST is 5361. This means T = 1, E = 5, A = 3, M = 7 and S = 6. SULK must be 6924, meaning U = 9, L = 2 and K = 4. This leaves LIKE, which is 2845, so I = 8. The code can be shown is this diagram:

A	E	I	K	L	M	S	T	U
3	5	8	4	2	7	6	1	9

41 **5361** is EAST
42 **1537** is TEAM
43 **2845** is LIKE
44 **6924** is SULK
45 **7824** is MILK
46 **SEAT**
47 **April** The twentieth letter of the alphabet is 'T' so Poppy's birthday must be in August. Her brother's birthday must be April, which is eight months after August.
48 **CRAWL**
49 **GRAIN**
50 **DARTS**

51–55 Use grids as shown below to help work out the missing word.

51 **TRAP**

	4	3	1
L	E	N	D

			2
A	L	S	O

	4	3	1
S	P	A	T

			2
F	O	U	R

52 **RISK**

	2		4
R	O	S	E

3			1
S	O	U	L

	2		4
M	I	L	K

3			1
S	O	A	R

53 **PAST**

	2		1
K	I	N	D

		3	4
L	A	C	E

	2		1
W	A	S	P

		3	4	
M	I	S	T	

54 **WAVE**

1	2		
P	E	A	K

		3	4
M	E	A	T

1	2		
W	A	I	T

		3	4	
H	I	V	E	

55 **RIVAL**

3		2		
W	R	O	T	E

5	4	1		
R	E	L	A	Y

3		2		
V	E	I	N	S

5	4	1		
L	A	R	C	H

56 **share**
57 **thrust**
58 **voice**
59 **clean**
60 **swift**
61 **TW** In this sequence each letter in the first pair moves forward by two places in the second pair.
62 **CH** In this sequence the first letter moves back by one place; the second letter moves forward by one place.
63 **NS** In this sequence the first letter moves forward by two places; the second letter moves forward by three places.
64 **QR** In this sequence each letter moves back by two places.
65 **RE** In this sequence the first letter in each pair moves forward by three places; the second letter moves back by two places.

66–70 Refer to Paper 2 Questions 47–51 on completing this type of question.
66 **justify, explain** 'Justify' and 'explain' are closest in meaning as both mean to 'give reasons'.
67 **common, ordinary** 'Common' and 'ordinary' are closest in meaning as both mean 'normal' or typical'.
68 **flood, overflow** 'Flood' and 'overflow' are closest in meaning as both refer to the effect of liquid exceeding the capacity of a container and flowing freely.
69 **stale, old** 'Stale' and 'old' are closest in meaning as both can refer to something that is 'past its best'.
70 **wreck, destroy** 'Wreck' and 'destroy' are closest in meaning as both mean to 'devastate' or 'shatter'.
71 **able, life**
72 **pot, frail**
73 **stale, brush**
74 **raft, cup**
75 **grin, neat**

76–80 Arrange the words in a grid to make it easier to put them in the correct alphabetical order.
76 **arrest, arrogant, artful, artificial, artistic**

a	r	r	e	s	t				
a	r	r	o	g	a	n	t		
a	r	t	f	u	l				
a	r	t	i	f	i	c	i	a	l
a	r	t	i	s	t	i	c		

77 exhibit, exhilarate, exile, expand, expectancy

e	x	h	i	b	i	t			
e	x	h	i	l	a	r	a	t	e
e	x	i	l	e					
e	x	p	a	n	d				
e	x	p	e	c	t	a	n	c	y

78 reason, reassure, rebel, rebuild, recite

r	e	a	s	o	n		
r	e	a	s	s	u	r	e
r	e	b	e	l			
r	e	b	u	i	l	d	
r	e	c	i	t	e		

79 illegible, illicit, illogical, illusion, illustrate

i	l	l	e	g	i	b	l	e	
i	l	l	i	c	i	t			
i	l	l	o	g	i	c	a	l	
i	l	l	u	s	i	o	n		
i	l	l	u	s	t	r	a	t	e

80 force, forcible, forecast, foreign, forever

f	o	r	c	e			
f	o	r	c	i	b	l	e
f	o	r	e	c	a	s	t
f	o	r	e	i	g	n	
f	o	r	e	v	e	r	

Paper 11 (pages 45–49)

1–6 Refer to Paper 6 Questions 51–55 on how to complete this type of question.

1 **FILE, FILL**
2 **FIST, MIST**
3 **SEAR, SEAL**
4 **HERB, HERD**
5 **LICE, VICE**
6 **RACE, FACE**

7–10 Refer to Paper 2 Questions 32–36 on how to answer this type of question.

7 **pet, eat, overweight**
8 **travel, rocket, astronauts**
9 **teacher, report, improve**
10 **cards, cats, dog**
11 **note** notepad, notebook, notepaper, noteworthy
12 **over** overcome, overcast, overall, overgrown
13 **flash** flashback, flashbulb, flashcard, flashlight
14 **bath** bathroom, bathrobe, bathtub, bathwater
15 **under** understanding, underline, underground, underfoot
16 **cheat**
17 **tale**
18 **sore**
19 **dart**
20 **paired**
21 **wail** Change the third letter from 'l' to 'i'.
22 **than** Replace the first letter with the third and fourth letters. The second letter then becomes the third letter. Change the last letter to 'n'.
23 **best** Add 's' before the final letter.
24 **mate** Swap the first and third letters.
25 **stop** The third and fourth letters become the first and second letters. The second letter becomes the third letter. The first letter becomes the fourth letter.
26 **leg** An 'ankle' joins the leg to the 'foot', just as a 'wrist' joins the 'arm' to the hand.
27 **serious** 'Serious' is a synonym of 'solemn', just as 'delighted' is a synonym of 'pleased'.
28 **outrageous** 'Outrageous' is an antonym of 'reasonable', just as 'sugary' is an antonym of 'sour'.
29 **edge** 'Edge' is a synonym of 'margin', just as 'cost' is a synonym of 'fee'.
30 **reluctantly** 'Reluctantly' is an antonym of 'readily', just as 'silence' is an antonym of 'clamour'.

31–34 Give two marks for each correct crossword.

31–32

	S		R		R
U	P	S	I	D	E
	R		D		P
M	E	D	D	L	E
	A		L		A
A	D	V	E	R	T

33–34

	S		A		N
S	T	A	P	L	E
	A		P		A
D	I	G	E	S	T
	N		A		L
O	S	P	R	E	Y

35–40 Begin with the letter 'C' which is in first, second and third positions, so C = 4. This means COAL = 4216, ECHO = 5432 and LACE = 6145. This means that HALO = 3162 as this is the only code remaining. Place the letters of the word below the numbers to make coding and decoding easier:

1	4	5	3	6	2
A	C	E	H	L	O

35 **5432** is ECHO
36 **4216** is COAL
37 **3162** is HALO
38 **6145** is LACE
39 **1435** is ACHE
40 **3265** is HOLE
41 **SE, WI** In this sequence each letter moves forward by one place.
42 **II, ME** In this sequence the first letter in each pair moves forward by two places; the second letter moves back by two places.
43 **DS, ER** In this sequence the first letter in each pair moves forward by one place; the second letter moves back by one place.
44 **31, 40** Each number in the sequence increases by 3.
45 **56, 61** This sequence is +5, -3, +5, -3 etc.
46 **negotiate, discuss** Both words mean to 'confer'.
47 **support, assist** Both words mean to 'help' or 'provide aid'.
48 **peace, calm** Both words mean 'ease' or 'contentment'.
49 **determined, persistent** Both words mean 'resolute' or 'unwavering'.
50 **Tomorrow is Saturday.** For this question you can only judge what is true based on the information given. The only relevant sentence is 'Yesterday is Thursday'. As yesterday was Thursday, today must be Friday and tomorrow Saturday.
51 **sh** mash, shelf
52 **ma** drama, manage
53 **gh** enough, ghost
54 **te** private, telephone
55 **se** please, second
56 **flight** 'Flight' is linked with 'transport' and 'aviation' and is also another word for a rapid 'exit' or 'fleeing'.
57 **trim** 'Trim' can mean 'slim' or 'slender' and can also (as a verb) mean to 'prune' or 'crop'.
58 **notice** 'Notice' is another word for an 'advert' or 'flyer' and can also (as a verb) mean to 'observe' or 'see'.
59 **draw** 'Draw' can refer to a 'tie' or 'stalemate', particularly in sport or any other type of competition, and can also mean (as a verb) to 'trace' or 'sketch'.
60 **air** 'Air' can mean to 'express' or 'show' (e,g, to 'air a grievance') and can also mean to 'ventilate' or 'freshen' (e.g. to 'air a room').
61 **nurse, medicine** The other three words are connected with illness.
62 **boredom, indifference** The other three words refer to interest or participation in something.
63 **glass, cup** The other three words are names of drinks.
64 **hunger, starving** The other three words refer to ways of eating.
65 **robin, ostrich** The other three words are parts of a bird's body.
66 **ARCH** SEARCHING
67 **LOCK** BLOCKED
68 **REST** INTERESTING
69 **TURN** RETURNED
70 **PORT** IMPORTANT
71 **panting**
72 **pasty**
73 **port**
74 **sight**
75 **quit**
76 **DEPART, PARTED**
77 **REMIT, MERIT**
78 **SEVER, VERSE**
79 **RETRACE, CATERER**
80 **HORSE, SHORE**

Paper 12 (pages 50–54)

1 **h** batch, heap; pitch, heave
2 **d** deed, damp; fond, deter
3 **t** malt, task; fact, tusk
4 **b** club, blunt; crab, brim
5 **n** even, neon; wean, noble
6 **r** stair, roam; flour, rent
7–9 Arrange the words in a grid to make it easier to put them in the correct alphabetical order.
7 **3421**

3	E	L	B	I	S	I	V	N	I	
4	E	L	B	I	S	S	O	P	M	I
2	E	L	B	I	D	E	N	I		
1	E	L	B	B	U	B				

8 **1342**

1	E	C	I	U	J					
3	E	S	I	U	R	B				
4	E	S	I	U	R	C				
2	E	C	N	A	S	I	U	N		

9 **3124**

3	G	N	I	P	O	H			
1	G	N	I	K	A	M			
2	G	N	I	K	A	W			
4	G	N	I	V	I	R	D		

10 C Begin with the fact that A must be second in the queue. Next, E must be fourth and D fifth. Since B is at the front, C must be third (in the middle).

11 **6** 3 + 1 + 2 = 6

12 **16** 3 + 1 + 7 + 5 = 16 (G is the 7th letter in the alphabet, so its value will be 7. E is the 5th letter, so its value will be 5.)

13 **11** 2 + 5 + 4 = 11 (D is the 4th letter in the alphabet, so its value will be 4.)

14–17 Give two marks for each correct crossword.

14–15

D	E	W
O	W	E
G	E	T

16–17

S	U	M
E	R	A
E	N	D

18–20 To get from the word to the code, count the distance from the beginning and/or end of the alphabet (e.g. 'C' is the third letter, so the code for 'C' is the third letter from the end, which is 'X'). To speed up the process, write the alphabet forwards, then backwards in a chart:

Word:	A	B	C	D	E	F	G	H	I	J	K	L	M
	N	O	P	Q	R	S	T	U	V	W	X	Y	Z
Code:	Z	Y	X	W	V	U	T	S	R	Q	P	O	N
	M	L	K	J	I	H	G	F	E	D	C	B	A

18 **XLG**

19 **MVZG**

20 **URHS**

21–24 Refer to Paper 2 Questions 47–51 on completing this type of question.

21 **appear, vanish** 'Appear' is most opposite to 'vanish' as 'appear' means to 'come into sight', whereas 'vanish' means to 'disappear from sight'.

22 **variety, routine** 'Variety' is most opposite to 'routine' as 'variety' means something that is 'varied', whereas 'routine' means 'a sequence of actions regularly followed'.

23 **ready, unprepared** 'Ready' is the most opposite to 'unprepared' as 'ready' means something is organised and available for use', whereas 'unprepared' means 'not ready or prepared for use'.

24 **treasured, ignored** 'Treasured' is the most opposite to 'ignored' as 'treasured' means 'thought highly of' as it is valued, whereas 'ignored' means 'disregarded' as it is considered unimportant.

25 **Not all dogs have name tags.** For this question you can only judge what is true based on the information given. The two sentences say that whilst 'Most dogs wear a collar', only 'Some dogs have a name tag'. The word 'some' implies that 'not all dogs have name tags'. There is no evidence for the other three potential answers.

26 **SERVE**

27 **UNITE**

28 **NEEDS**

29 **THREAD**

30 **LAMP**

31 **beginning, ending** The 'first' is found at the 'beginning' as the 'last' is found at the 'ending'.

32 **croaks, roars** A frog 'croaks' as a lion 'roars'.

33 **maximum, heavy** 'Maximum' is the opposite of 'minimum', as 'heavy' is the opposite of 'light'.

34 **children, women** The plural of 'child' is 'children', as the plural of 'woman' is 'women'.

35 **trustworthy, threaten** 'Trustworthy' is the opposite of 'dishonest', as 'threaten' is the opposite of 'protect'.

36–40 Use grids as shown below to help work out the missing word.

36 **EARN**

	3	1	
P	I	N	T

	2	4	
P	A	L	E

	3	1	
T	R	E	E

	2	4	
T	A	N	K

37 **BOIL**

1		4	
R	A	M	P

	2	3	
B	O	A	T

1		4	
B	U	L	L

	2	3	
C	O	I	N

38 **DOWN**

		3	4
P	U	R	E

1	2		
W	I	S	P

		3	4
Y	A	W	N

1	2		
D	O	T	E

39 **TIER**

	3	2		
C	L	O	A	K

1			4	
M	O	D	E	L

	3	2		
W	E	I	G	H

1			4	
T	H	I	R	D

40 **LOFT**

	4	2	
W	E	A	N

1			3
S	E	L	F

	4	2	
S	T	O	P

1			3
L	E	A	F

41 **BAND** ABANDONED
42 **FORM** INFORMED
43 **LIST** CYCLISTS
44 **WARD** REWARDING
45 **MINT** BADMINTON
46 **aeroplane, car** The other three words are names of jobs or careers.
47 **lake, harbour** The other three words are geographical *land* features.
48 **begin, start** The other three words are concerned with halting something.
49 **compassionate, charitable** The other three words are concerned with unpleasant or unkind traits.
50 **rubbish, insects** The other three words are group nouns (e.g. a litter of kittens, a herd of cows, a swarm of insects).
51 **dairy, diary** Writing in a diary is a good way to remember special occasions.
52 **hits, goals** When you are playing football, the aim is to score as many goals as possible.
53 **adults, children** Do not leave very young children unsupervised with a dog.
54 **sum, word** You can use your dictionary to find out what a word means.
55 **toy, pet** A guinea pig is a small animal, often kept as a pet.
56 **exist**
57 **stroke**
58 **value**
59 **weary**
60 **mince**
61 **gentle, calm** 'Gentle' is a synonym of 'calm', as 'ideal' is a synonym of 'perfect'.
62 **cold, unfriendly** 'Cold' is a synonym of 'unfriendly' as 'immense' is a synonym of 'enormous'.
63 **graceful, ballerina** An 'athlete' can be described as 'sporty', as a 'ballerina' can be described as 'graceful'.
64 **prevent, allow** 'Prevent' is an antonym of 'allow', as 'ignore' is an antonym of 'notice'.
65–69 Begin with the letter 'y' which ends two words and begins the other, so is 2. Thus YEAR = 2415, meaning E = 4, A = 1 AND R = 5. Since E = 4, it is now simple to work out that DEFY = 6472 and OBEY = 8342. The code can be shown in a chart:

A	B	D	E	F	O	R	Y
1	3	6	4	7	8	5	2

65 **6472** is DEFY
66 **8342** is OBEY
67 **2415** is YEAR
68 **BODY**
69 **BREAD**
70 **IMB** The first and third letters in each set move forward by one place and the second letter moves back by one place.
71 **YTM** Each letter in the first set moves forward by two places in the second set.
72 **WV** This is a 'mirror' pattern: imagine a mirror line between 'M' and 'N' in the alphabet. 'D' is the fourth letter from the beginning, so will change into the fourth letter from the end ('W'); 'E' is the fifth letter from the beginning, so will change into the fifth letter from the end ('V').
73 **NUJ** Each letter in the first set moves back by one place in the second set.
74 **YV**Refer to Question 72. 'B' is the second letter in the alphabet, so will change into the second letter from the end ('Y'); 'E' is the fifth letter in the alphabet, so will change into the fifth from the end ('V').
75 **GI, PR** In this sequence the letters in each pair move forward by three places.
76 **BX, JP** In this sequence the first letter in each pair moves forward by two places; the second letter moves back by two places.
77 **UF, TG** In this sequence the first letter in each pair moves back by one place; the second letter moves forward by one place.
78 **33, 48** The sequence is +3, +6, +9, +12, +15.
79 **18, 13** There are two sequences which alternate. In both sequences the numbers decrease by 1 each time. In the first sequence is 19, 18, 17. The second sequence is 15, 14, 13.
80 **26, 32** Each the number in the sequence increases by 6.

Paper 13 (pages 54–58)

1 **tricky, faithful** 'Tricky' is a synonym of 'complicated', as 'faithful' is a synonym of 'loyal'.
2 **reward, punishment** 'Reward' is a synonym of 'prize', as 'penalty' is a synonym of 'punishment'.
3 **reject, accept** 'Reject' means to 'deny inclusion', as 'accept' means to 'allow inclusion''.
4 **wing, paw** A bat has 'wings' as a rabbit has 'paws'.
5 **invented, actual** 'Invented' is a synonym of 'imaginary', as 'actual' is a synonym of 'real'.
6 **ban**
7 **have**
8 **slash**
9 **cave**
10 **path**

11–15 Refer to Paper 2 Questions 47–51 on completing this type of question.

11 **reaction, response** 'Reaction' and 'response' are closest in meaning as both words describe the act of 'responding' to something or someone.

12 **spread, expand** 'Spread' and 'expand' are closest in meaning as both words can mean to 'extend a surface area'.

13 **fix, repair** 'Fix' and 'repair' are closest in meaning as both words mean to 'correct a fault or breakage'.

14 **degree, amount** 'Degree' and 'amount' are closest in meaning as both words mean the 'size' or 'quantity' of something.

15 **hole, opening** 'Hole' and 'opening' are closest in meaning as both words mean an 'aperture' or 'gap'.

16–20 Refer to Paper 1 Questions 50–54 on how to complete this type of question.

16 **15, 13** The sequence is -2, +5, -2, +5 etc.

17 **29, 64** Each number in the sequence increases by 7.

18 **8, 8** There are two sequences which alternate. In the first sequence, starting with 2, the numbers increase by 2 each time (2, 4, 6, 8). In the second sequence, starting with 4, the numbers increase by 4 each time (4, 8, 12).

19 **49, 64** The sequence is of the square numbers in the times tables ($3 \times 3 = 9$; $4 \times 4 = 16$; $5 \times 5 = 25$ and so on), or the number added increases by 2 each time: +7, +9, +11, +13, +15, +17.

20 **20, 25** Each number in the sequence increases by 5.

21 **Jacob, Henry, Harry, Fred** A table is the easiest way to sort the information, like this:

	Science	Maths	Art	Spanish	French	History	Geography	Drama
Claire	✓	✓						
Amy	✓	✓						
Harry						✓	✓	✓
Fred						✓	✓	✓
Jacob			✓	✓				✓
Henry			✓	✓				✓
Amelia					✓			
Ravi		✓					✗	✓

22–24 Refer to Paper 5 Questions 61–65 on how to answer this type of question.

22 **VDYH** To get from the word to the code, move each letter forwards three places.

23 **OGURCIG** To get from the word to the code, move the first letter forward two places, move the second letter back two places, move the third letter forward two places, move the fourth letter back two places, etc.

24 **WINDY** To get from the code to the word, move the first letter back by two places, the second letter back by three places, the third letter back by four places, etc. To work out what letter 'E' stands for, use the alphabet in a loop: WXYZABCDE.

25 **Crows lay eggs.** For this question you can only judge what is true based on the information given. As 'crows are birds' and 'birds lay eggs' it must be true that 'crows lay eggs'. There is no evidence in the given sentences to support the other three options.

26 **st** almost, start

27 **te** excite, temper

28 **me** frame, melon

29 **pe** shape, permit

30 **er** whisper, erupt

31–35 Refer to Paper 2 Questions 27-31 on how to complete this type of question.

31 **11** Add 1 to the left-hand number OR subtract 2 from the right-hand number (the answer will be the same): $10 + 1 = 11$, $13 - 2 = 11$

32 **8** Divide the right-hand number by the left-hand number: $32 \div 4 = 8$

33 **7 11** Add 5 to the left-hand number OR subtract 5 from the right-hand number (the answer will be the same): $2 + 5 = 7$, $12 - 5 = 7$

34 **9** Subtract 3 from the left-hand number or subtract 1 from the right-hand number: both equations will give the same answer for the middle number.

35 **9** Divide the left-hand number by the right-hand number: $27 \div 3 = 9$.

36 **patch** Add the letters 'ch' to the end of the word.

37 **weak** The last letter becomes the second letter.

38 **in** Remove the first, second and final letters.

39 **ate**The last two letters become the first two letters and the second letter becomes the last letter.

40 **bark** Change the last letter from 'e' to 'k'.

41 **last** 'Last' means the 'final' or 'latest'; it also means to 'continue' or 'go on'.

42 **needle** A 'needle' has a sharp point, as does a 'thorn' and a 'quill'; 'needle' can also mean to 'annoy' or 'pester'.

43 **land** 'Land' means 'earth' or 'ground'; it also means to 'arrive' or 'come down'.

44 **state** 'State' means to 'explain' or 'say'; it can also mean the 'condition' or 'phase' of something.
45 **tough** 'Tough' means 'strong' or 'firm', and also 'stern' or 'strict'.
46 **b** risk, bowl
47 **r** band, harm
48 **l** fame, camel
49 **d** boar, draw
50 **e** ton, mean
51 **PL, SI** The first letter in each pair moves forward by three places; the second letter moves back by three places.
52 **CX, FU** The first letter in each pair moves forward by one place; the second letter moves back by one place.
53 **UE, SG** The first letter in each pair moves back by two places, then forward by one place, and so on. The second letter moves forward by two places, then back by one place, and so on.
54 **MN, UV** In this sequence pairs of letters are consecutive in the alphabet, e.g. MN, OP, QR etc.
55–60 The letter R is the key to solving this code. It appears as first letter twice, third letter once and fourth letter once. Therefore R = 6. This means that DARE = 2463 and OVER = 5736. As O = 5 we can work out that ROAD = 6542, leaving REAL = 6341. The full code can be shown in a chart:

A	D	E	L	O	R	V
4	2	3	1	5	6	7

55 **6341** is REAL
56 **6542** is ROAD
57 **2463** is DARE
58 **5736** is OVER
59 **ORDER**
60 **DROVE**
61–65 Use the grids as shown below to help work out the missing word.
61 **POST**

2	1		
A	R	M	Y

3		4	
C	H	E	W

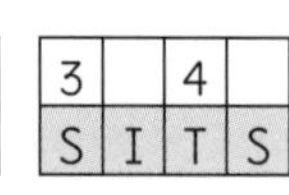

2	1		
O	P	E	N

3		4	
S	I	T	S

62 **FERN**

		2	1
S	L	A	P

		3	4
H	E	L	M

		2	1
R	E	E	F

		3	4
B	A	R	N

63 **EVER**

3			1	
C	H	I	R	P

		2		4
P	R	I	C	E

3			1	
E	L	D	E	R

		2		4
D	I	V	E	R

64 **PINE**

	4		1
R	E	I	N

2	3			
O	T	T	E	R

	4		1
R	E	A	P

2	3		
I	N	C	H

65 **SAVE**

	3	4	
G	A	M	E

	2	1	
B	O	R	E

	3	4	
O	V	E	N

	2	1	
F	A	S	T

66 **MEAN**
67 **TEAM**
68 **DARE**
69 **STAR**
70 **THROB**
71–74 Give two marks for each correct crossword.
71–72

B	A	R
E	G	O
G	O	T

73–74

T	I	N
A	C	E
P	E	T

75 **wolf, howl** 'Howl' is a sound made by a 'wolf', as 'buzz' is the sound made by a 'bee'.
76 **grab, snatch** 'Grab' is a synonym of 'snatch', as 'rear' is a synonym of 'back'.
77 **crowded, deserted** 'Crowded' is an antonym of 'deserted', as 'crude' is an antonym of 'polite'.
78 **glass, glasses** 'Glasses' is the plural form of 'glass', as 'leaves' is the plural form of 'leaf'.
79 **damage, harm** 'Damage' is a synonym of 'harm', as 'tease' is a synonym of 'irritate'.
80 **wave, sea** A 'wave' can be seen on the 'sea', as a' star' can be seen in the 'sky'.

A B C D E F G H I J K L M N O P Q R S T U V W X Y Z

If the code for P L A T E is q m b u f, what are the codes for these words?

B 24

26 FORK ________

27 SPOON ________

28 CUP ________

What do these codes stand for?

29 l o j g f ________

30 t b v d f s ________

5

A, B, C, D and E are boats in a race. A is due south of C and due north west of B. D is west of A.

B 25

31 Which boat is furthest east? ________

1

Here are the number codes for four words. Match the right code to the right word.

B 24

PUSH	HOPS	CHAP	POUCH
2465	8236	6752	64782

32 PUSH ________

33 HOPS ________

34 CHAP ________

35 POUCH ________

36 Write CHOPS in code. ________

5

Underline the two words in each line which are most similar in type or meaning.

B 5

	Example	dear	pleasant	poor	extravagant	expensive
37	coward	guilty	courage	bravery	tough	remedy
38	face	glance	prevent	permit	look	suggest
39	traffic	lights	halt	car	road	stop
40	cross	stingy	generous	angry	loving	wealthy
41	red	paper	paint	tint	artist	colour

5

Complete the following sentences in the best way by choosing one word from each set of brackets.

B 15

Example Tall is to (tree, short, colour) as narrow is to (thin, white, wide).

42 Short is to (shirt, maximum, brief) as incredible is to (believable, edible, amazing).

43 Pear is to (fruit, tree, pair) as cabbage is to (soup, vegetable, sprout).

44 Ear is to (ring, listening, noticed) as mouth is to (head, lips, tasting).

45 Vigorous is to (active, athlete, feeble) as sympathy is to (crying, upset, pity).

46 Tough is to (fragile, strict, harmless) as save is to (money, earn, squander).

5

Find two letters which will end the first word and start the second word.

Example rea (c h) air

47 soot (___ ___) althy

48 up (___ ___) ce

49 offi (___ ___) real

50 circ (___ ___) ual

51 pla (___ ___) vent

B 10

5

Rearrange the muddled letters in capitals to make a proper word. The answer will complete the sentence sensibly.

Example A BEZAR is an animal with stripes. ZEBRA

52 A NORIB is a type of bird. ___________

53 Films are shown in a AMNICE. ___________

54 A GIMANIAC does tricks with cards. ___________

55 A LAECM doesn't need much water. ___________

56 CEMNOCME means to begin. ___________

B 16

5

Give the two missing numbers in the following sequences.

Example 2 4 6 8 10 12

57 75 28 70 32 ___ ___ 60

58 6 12 18 ___ ___ 36 42

59 73 75 79 ___ 93 ___ 115

60 175 150 ___ 100 75 ___ 25

61 6 8 9 12 ___ ___ 15

B 23

5

Rearrange the letters in capitals to make another word. The new word has something to do with the first two words.

Example spot soil SAINT STAIN

62 turn swirl PINS ___________

63 quay jetty RIPE ___________

64 platform phase GATES ___________

65 deceive trick TEACH ___________

66 snare catch PART ___________

B 16

5

Change one word so that the sentence makes sense. Underline the word you are taking out and write your new word on the line.

B 14

Example I waited in line to buy a book to see the film. ticket

67 The shortest day of the year is February. ____________

68 I reserved a chair for two at the restaurant. ____________

69 Her father complained that the telephone bill was too cheap. ____________

70 The kitten scratched our new chair with her tail. ____________

71 She boiled just enough tea in the kettle to make a hot drink. ____________

5

Find and underline the two words which need to change places for each sentence to make sense.

B 17

Example She went to letter the write.

72 Was which year in the big storm?

73 It is important that form each is filled in completely.

74 From friends some Australia are visiting.

75 We picked on shells up the beach.

76 I made that I have admit a mistake.

5

Fill in the crosswords so that all the given words are included. You have been given one letter as a clue in each crossword.

B 19

77–78

■		■		■	
■		■	S	■	
■		■		■	

defuse, pavers, assets, cheers, disuse, lavish

79–80

■		■		■	
■		■		■	
W					
■		■		■	

whiter, drench, bitten, search, bother, docile

4

Now go to the Progress Chart to record your score! Total 80

Paper 8

Complete the following expressions by underlining the missing word.

B 15

Example Frog is to tadpole as swan is to (duckling, baby, <u>cygnet</u>).

1 Butterfly is to caterpillar as frog is to (pond, tadpole, croak).

2 Vacant is to occupied as mean is to (selfish, person, kind).

3 Clock is to hands as piano is to (music, keys, instrument).

4 Fair is to just as imply is to (order, suggest, request).

5 Fact is to fiction as import is to (purchase, sell, export).

5

Find a word that can be put in front of each of the following words to make new, compound words.

B 11

Example	cast	fall	ward	pour	<u>*down*</u>
6	cress	colour	fall	melon	________
7	lady	mark	slide	lord	________
8	light	break	dream	time	________
9	coat	bow	drop	fall	________
10	fall	burn	mill	break	________

5

Underline the word in the brackets which goes best with the words outside the brackets.

B 1

Example word, paragraph, sentence (pen, cap, <u>letter,</u> top, stop)

11 daffodil, poppy, tulip (stem, plant, snowdrop, grow, garden)

12 shriek, howl, roar (sound, whisper, wail, conversation, noise)

13 climb, rise, ascend (shrink, arrive, movement, soar, descend)

14 autumn, winter, summer (year, Easter, calendar, spring, season)

15 hail, sleet, snow (thunder, rain, drought, wet, weather)

5

Find the three-letter word which can be added to the letters in capitals to make a new word. The new word will complete the sentence sensibly.

B 22

Example The cat sprang onto the MO. <u>*USE*</u>

16 What shall we do to CELEBE your birthday? ________

17 I must stop CHEG my pencil. ________

18 The picture was very COLFUL. ________

19 My parents can both ATD Sports Day. ________

20 It's hard to BRHE whilst swimming under water. ________

5

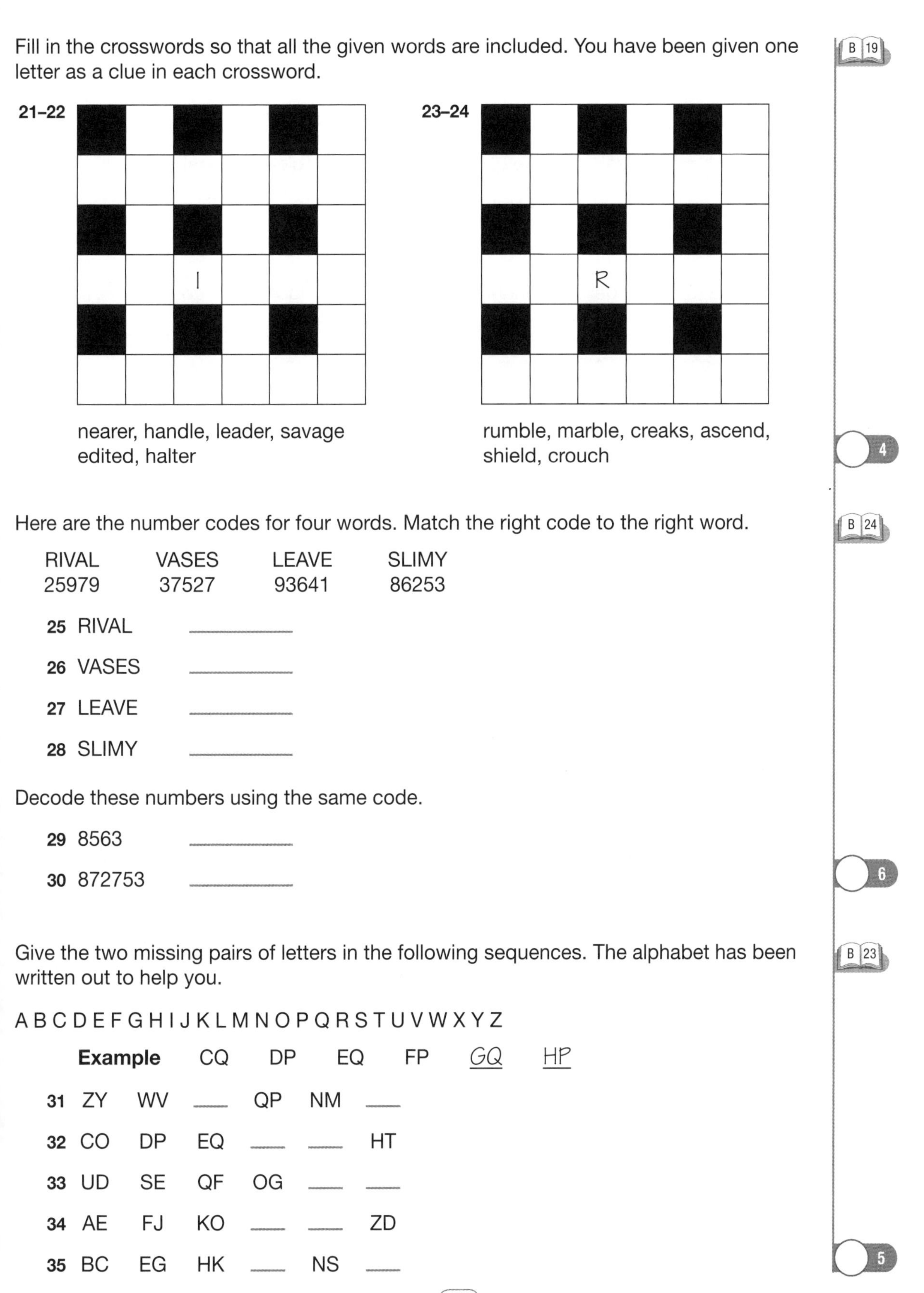

Fill in the crosswords so that all the given words are included. You have been given one letter as a clue in each crossword.

B 19

21–22

nearer, handle, leader, savage edited, halter

23–24

rumble, marble, creaks, ascend, shield, crouch

4

Here are the number codes for four words. Match the right code to the right word.

B 24

RIVAL	VASES	LEAVE	SLIMY
25979	37527	93641	86253

25 RIVAL __________

26 VASES __________

27 LEAVE __________

28 SLIMY __________

Decode these numbers using the same code.

29 8563 __________

30 872753 __________

6

Give the two missing pairs of letters in the following sequences. The alphabet has been written out to help you.

B 23

A B C D E F G H I J K L M N O P Q R S T U V W X Y Z

Example CQ DP EQ FP GQ HP

31 ZY WV ___ QP NM ___

32 CO DP EQ ___ ___ HT

33 UD SE QF OG ___ ___

34 AE FJ KO ___ ___ ZD

35 BC EG HK ___ NS ___

5

Underline the one word which **cannot be made** from the letters of the word in capital letters.

B 7

Example STATIONERY stone tyres ration <u>nation</u> noisy

36 BREAKABLE	bleak	area	leer	bleed	rabble
37 POTATOES	state	tests	soap	taste	post
38 CONTROVERSY	strove	sorry	overstay	very	store
39 BELONGINGS	singe	longing	ginger	lobes	gongs
40 DREADFUL	fared	leader	flared	deaf	ladder

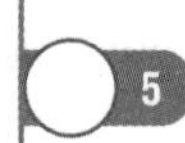

Complete the following sentences by selecting the most sensible word from each group of words given in the brackets. Underline the words selected.

Example The (<u>children</u>, books, foxes) carried the (houses, <u>books</u>, steps) home from the (greengrocer, <u>library</u>, factory).

41 The cake was (burnt, frozen, ready) because she was too late removing it from the (cupboard, oven, shop).

42 (Happy, Energetic, Tired) children who don't get enough (food, sleep, drink) find it hard to concentrate at (home, play, school).

43 The (hamster, dog, horse) stayed in the (kennel, nest, den) while it was (windy, raining, playing) outside.

44 Read the (question, reply, word), then carefully (imagine, guess, plan) your (answer, problem, subject).

45 Everyone was (sad, pleased, hurt) that we had a great (holiday, birthday, marriage) that (night, season, summer).

Find the letter which will complete both pairs of words, ending the first word and starting the second. The same letter must be used for both pairs of words.

Example mea (<u>t</u>) able fi (<u>t</u>) ub

46 bar	(___)	ettle	wal	(___)	now
47 bea	(___)	est	gri	(___)	ose
48 fac	(___)	ase	sal	(___)	ast
49 ro	(___)	old	com	(___)	lack
50 for	(___)	ask	war	(___)	ent

Look at the first group of three words. The word in the middle has been made from the other two words. Complete the second group of three words in the same way, making a new word in the middle.

Example PAIN INTO TOOK ALSO SOON ONLY

51	BOWL	BORE	READ	HARD	______	VEST
52	HINT	THAW	WEAK	OPEN	______	EASY
53	TIED	DONE	FRONT	LIMP	______	STALE
54	BALL	WELL	WEIRD	LEAN	______	MOIST
55	PRAYS	CHAP	PATCH	ROAST	______	WRIST

DESIRE DESCRIBE DESPAIR DESERVE DESCEND

If these words were placed in alphabetical order, which one would come:

56 fourth? ______

57 first? ______

58 second? ______

A B C D and E are five cars in a race.

C finishes three minutes ahead of E.

D takes fifteen minutes to complete the race, which is three minutes slower than E.

A wins the race, beating C by two minutes and B by four minutes.

59 Which car comes last? ______

60 How many minutes does C take to complete the race? ______

If s = 1, t = 2, u = 3, v = 4, w = 5 and x = 6, find the value of the following.

61 $(t \times u) + s =$ ______

62 $\frac{x}{u} =$ ______

63 $(w \times v) \div t =$ ______

64 $u \times u =$ ______

Read the first two statements and then underline one of the four options below that must be true.

65 'Gold is a metal. Rings can be made of gold.'

Rings are always made of metal.

Rings are usually made of gold.

Rings can be made of metal.

Gold is an expensive metal.

Underline the pair of words most opposite in meaning.

B 9

Example	cup, mug	coffee, milk	hot, cold
66	vague, certain	coarse, rough	modern, new
67	fall, drop	purchase, buy	scatter, collect
68	satisfy, disappoint	scare, panic	promise, pledge
69	provide, supply	undermine, enhance	advice, recommendation
70	bronze, copper	nervous, stressed	unusual, ordinary

5

Underline two words, one from each group, that go together to form a new word. The word in the first group always comes first.

B 8

Example	(hand, green, for)	(light, house, sure)
71	(out, in, wide)	(light, sect, part)
72	(through, in, though)	(sign, full, out)
73	(what, we, no)	(mad, lie, at)
74	(all, at, in)	(track, together, tempt)
75	(act, be, leg)	(for, am, all)

5

A B C D E F G H I J K L M N O P Q R S T U V W X Y Z

Solve the problems by working out the letter codes.

B 24

76 If the code for JURY is HSPW, what is the code for CORAL? ________

77 If the code for SHARP is UJCTR, what is the code for ALIBI? ________

78 If the code for PLANK is LHWJG, what does the code NECDP mean? ________

79 If the code for MINCE is NKQGJ, what is the code for HARBOUR? ________

80 If the code for FOUR is GNVQ, what is the code for ARCH? ________

5

Now go to the Progress Chart to record your score! **Total** **80**

Paper 9

Underline the two words on each line which are made from the same letters.

B 7

Example	TAP	PET	TEA	POT	EAT	
1	METEOR	LAMENT	TREMOR	METAL	MENTAL	LATER
2	START	TASTE	STATE	PLEAT	TRAPS	TRUST
3	REWARD	FREE	DRAFT	DRAWER	REFER	WAFER
4	TRACT	CHEAT	CRATE	ACHE	REACT	RATE
5	STOAT	OATS	STORE	TOES	ROSE	TOAST

5

Underline the word in the brackets closest in meaning to the word in capitals.

B 5

Example UNHAPPY (unkind death laughter <u>sad</u> friendly)

6 QUANTITY (ingredients long cooking order amount)

7 RAMBLE (hiker stroll trail thorn path)

8 AWKWARD (graceful simple skilful false difficult)

9 GRAZE (knee fall scrape plaster skin)

10 FLAIR (secret lie truth talent whisper)

5

A B C D E F G H I J K L M N O P Q R S T U V W X Y Z

If Z M R R M K is the code for BOTTOM, what do these codes stand for?

B 24

11 R M K Z ____________

12 E P M S L B ____________

13 E Y P B C L ____________

What are the codes for the following words?

14 EARTH ____________

15 LOWEST ____________

5

Find the four-letter word hidden at the end of one word and the beginning of the next word. The order of the letters may not be changed.

B 21

Example The children had bats and balls. <u>sand</u>

16 The team did not win a single match this year. ____________

17 I hope I can have a brand new phone for my birthday. ____________

18 I do hope eleven pounds isn't too much to spend. ____________

19 She always helps out when needed. ____________

20 Money is also urgently needed by the charity. ____________

5

Underline the two words, one from each group, which are the most opposite in meaning.

B 9

Example (dawn, <u>early</u>, awake) (<u>late</u>, stop, sunrise)

21 (open, shut, near) (closed, almost, stop)

22 (trip, war, down) (battle, fall, peace)

23 (alert, bright, perfect) (awake, distracted, clever)

24 (deliberate, aim, hostile) (accidental, unfriendly, planned)

25 (secret, essential, locate) (discover, find, unimportant)

26 (flee, weekend, busy) (remain, walk, wander)

27 (happy, mad, complete) (sane, whole, joyful)

7

Read the first two statements and then underline one of the four options below that must be true.

B 25

28 'Many mammals are plant-eaters. Some mammals live in Africa.'

Some mammals live in herds.
Many plants are found only in Africa.
Some African mammals may feed on leaves.
Most of the animals in Africa are mammals.

Read the first two statements and then underline one of the four options below that must be true.

29 'Language is based on words. Letters are used for each sound in a word.'

Words are usually written.
Sounds can be represented by letters.
There are many different languages.
All languages use the same alphabet.

2

Fill in the crosswords so that all the given words are included. You have been given one letter as a clue in each crossword.

B 19

30–31

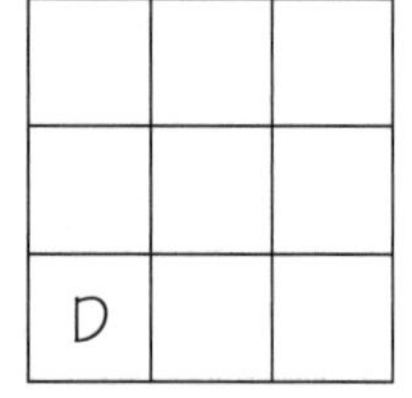

lap, pot, ego,
dot, led, ago

32–33

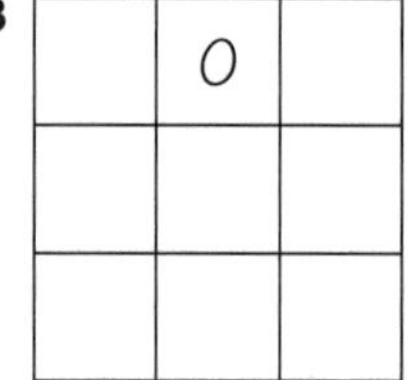

two, oar, eye,
way, ore, toe

34–35

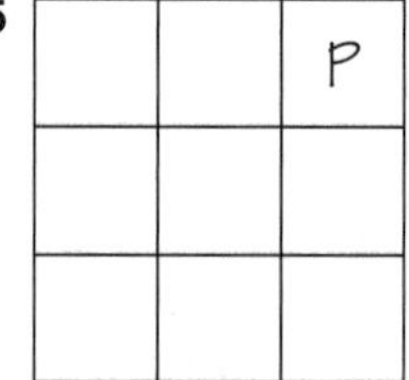

dam, ice, pet,
ace, met, dip

6

Give the two missing numbers in the following sequences.

B 23

Example	2	4	6	8	10	12	
36	3	___	9	12	___	18	21
37	7	9	13	19	___	___	49
38	___	42	31	22	___	10	7
39	6	___	___	30	38	46	54
40	14	36	21	30	___	___	35

5

Find two letters which will end the first word and start the second word.

B 10

Example rea (c h) air

41 cha (___ ___) vade
42 cau (___ ___) rious
43 norm (___ ___) ways
44 rememb (___ ___) ror
45 toa (___ ___) reet

5

Underline the two words which are the odd ones out in the following groups of words.

B 4

Example black king purple green house

46 metre litre centimetre kilometre kilogram

47 shout look whisper march talk

48 dull clear boring unexciting weather

49 London city country France town

50 promote encourage hinder boost depress

5

Underline the one word in the brackets which will go equally well with both the pairs of words outside the brackets.

B 5

Example rush, attack cost, fee (price, hasten, strike, charge, money)

51 stone, pebble sway, wobble (danger, rock, roll, hard, rough)

52 irritable, cross brisk, lively (touchy, sluggish, quick, snappy, hasty)

53 idea, knowledge agreement, pact (intelligence, understanding, cooperation, patient, acceptance)

54 division, group grade, course (collection, student, class, teacher, sort)

55 bud, flower grow, progress (plant, increase, movement, stem, blossom)

5

Change the first word of the third pair in the same way as the other pairs to give a new word.

B 18

Example bind, hind bare, hare but, hut

56 bit, bite kit, kite sit, ________

57 chill, hill shops, hops cover, ________

58 deed, feed dish, fish date, ________

59 file, life dire, ride, rise, ________

60 moth, hot with, hit mash, ________

5

Rearrange the letters in capitals to make another word. The new word has something to do with the first two words.

B 16

Example spot soil SAINT STAIN

61 dull dim DEAF ________

62 genuine true EARL ________

63 short quick FIBRE ________

64 violent fury GEAR ________

65 mistake oversight SEPAL ________

5

Complete the following sentences by selecting the most sensible word from each group of words given in the brackets. Underline the words selected.

B 14

Example The (children, books, foxes) carried the (houses, books, steps) home from the (greengrocer, library, factory).

66 We will (go, leave, listen) to the (cinema, holiday, moon) next (evening, week, day).

67 As (autumn, spring, winter) came the (leaves, petals, branches) began to (grow, develop, fall) from the trees.

68 You can take some (friends, money, clothes) to (play, spend, wear) with in the (bank, park, bath).

69 My (pets, parents, toys) go to bed after (watching, playing, counting) the (road, books, television).

70 A (clock, thermometer, radio) measures (temperature, time, sound) to the nearest (week, wave, second).

5

Here are the number codes for four words. Match the right code to the right word.

B 24

PEAR	AREA	SOAP	ROPE
7254	6243	4356	5635

71 PEAR ____________

72 AREA ____________

73 SOAP ____________

74 ROPE ____________

75 Write POSE in code. ____________

5

Change one word so that the sentence makes sense. Underline the word you are taking out and write your new word on the line.

B 14

Example I waited in line to buy a book to see the film. *ticket*

76 As it's Saturday tomorrow, you can get up late to watch the film. ____________

77 She spent her pocket money because she couldn't find anything tempting to buy. ____________

78 Brush your hair after eating so many sweets. ____________

79 Our cinema doesn't always show the most recent songs. ____________

80 She took a sip of her drink because she was hungry. ____________

5

Now go to the Progress Chart to record your score! **Total** 80

Paper 10

Give the two missing pairs of letters in the following sequences. The alphabet has been written out to help you.

B 23

A B C D E F G H I J K L M N O P Q R S T U V W X Y Z

Example	CQ	DP	EQ	FP	GQ	HP
1	JD	KE	LF	MG	___	___
2	AJ	BI	DG	GD	___	___
3	UB	PB	LD	___	GF	___
4	HT	GU	___	EW	DX	___
5	GV	HU	JS	KR	___	___

5

Choose two words, one from each set of brackets, to complete the sentences in the best way.

B 15

Example Smile is to happiness as (drink, tear, shout) is to (whisper, laugh, sorrow).

6 Uncle is to aunt as (husband, son, father) is to (grandmother, relative, wife).

7 Reveal is to show as (unite, copy, glance) is to (write, join, divide).

8 Lion is to den as (mouse, pig, bee) is to (stable, sty, sting).

9 Sad is to melancholy as (ghostly, spirited, lazy) is to (vigorous, calm, spiteful).

10 Depart is to arrive as (deny, agree, accept) is to (state, respond, admit).

5

Find the three-letter word which can be added to the letters in capitals to make a new word. The new word will complete the sentence sensibly.

B 22

Example The cat sprang onto the MO. USE

11 You can ARGE to have a friend to play next week. ________

12 She felt LLY once the other children had gone home. ________

13 The answer was explained CLLY. ________

14 Mum, Danika keeps RETING what I say! ________

15 The Halloween MS scared the younger children. ________

5

If $a = 6$, $b = 2$, $c = 0$, $d = 5$, $e = 10$, find the answer to these calculations.

B 26

16 $a + d + e =$ ___

17 $(be) \div d =$ ___

18 $(a \times b) + d =$ ___

19 $abc =$ ___

20 $(d \times e) \div (b \times d) =$ ___

5

Which one letter can be added to the front of all of these words to make new words?

B 12

Example care cat crate call

21	___eek	___ick	___core	___elf	___ack
22	___oyal	___ure	___uck	___ist	___oad
23	___ook	___oot	___orn	___our	___ost
24	___ire	___ice	___eed	___eal	___ale
25	___oad	___ool	___ent	___ank	___uck

5

Underline one word in the brackets which is most opposite in meaning to the word in capitals.

B 6

Example WIDE (broad vague long narrow motorway)

26 HOST (party hostess invite guest speak)

27 ENDLESS (close beginning limited boundary outcome)

28 CATCH (game grab try drop problem)

29 OBJECT (article focus purpose approve plan)

30 ARTIFICIAL (false reliable fake genuine environment)

5

Rearrange the muddled letters in capitals to make a proper word. The answer will complete the sentence sensibly.

B 16

Example A BEZAR is an animal with stripes. ZEBRA

31 Put a ATPMS on that before you post it! ______

32 His mother was ODUPR of his achievements. ______

33 I have ITENIVD everyone to my party. ______

34 The witness described the DICTENAC. ______

35 I lost my SERPU outside the bank. ______

5

Fill in the crosswords so that all the given words are included. You have been given one letter as a clue in each crossword.

B 19

36–37

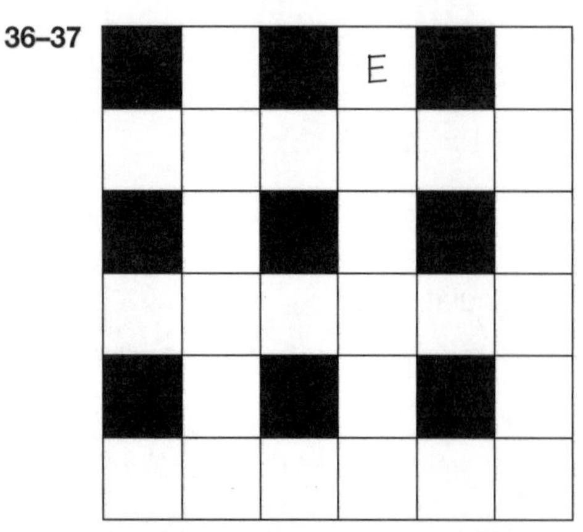

stodgy, matted, storey, editor, impart, amidst

38–39

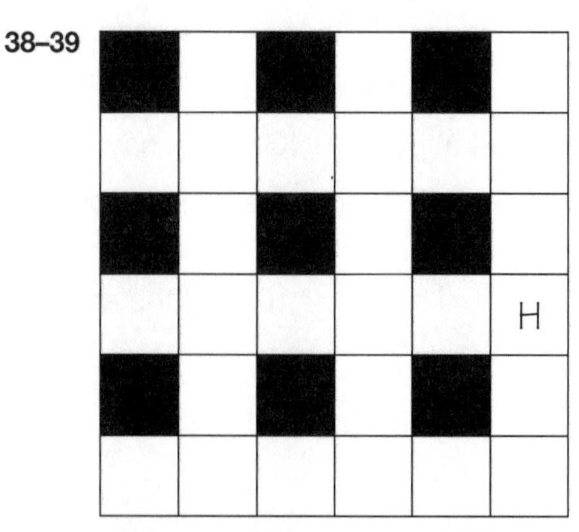

states, crutch, course, archer, censor, loiter

4

Read the first two statements and then underline one of the four options below that must be true.

B 25

40 'Tea is grown in China. Many people drink tea.'

Most people in China grow tea plants.

Tea is a more popular drink than coffee.

Some people drink Chinese tea.

Tea is a hot drink.

1

Here are the number codes for four words. Match the right code to the right word.

B 24

EAST	TEAM	LIKE	SULK
6924	1537	5361	2845

41 EAST ______

42 TEAM ______

43 LIKE ______

44 SULK ______

45 Write MILK in code. ______

46 Decode 6531. ______

6

Poppy's birthday is in the month which ends with the 20th letter of the alphabet. Her brother's birthday is eight months later.

B 25

47 In which month is Poppy's brother's birthday? ______

1

Underline the one word which **can be made** from the letters of the word in capital letters.

B 7

Example	CHAMPION	camping	notch	peach	cramp	<u>chimp</u>
48	CAULIFLOWER	lions	fault	relay	colder	crawl
49	FLAVOURING	reign	vowel	gravel	grain	float
50	STRAINED	timed	darts	stripe	earl	nested

3

Look at the first group of three words. The word in the middle has been made from the other two words. Complete the second group of three words in the same way, making a new word in the middle.

B 18

Example	PA<u>IN</u>	INTO	<u>TO</u>OK	ALSO	<u>SOON</u>	ONLY
51	LEND	DONE	ALSO	SPAT	______	FOUR
52	ROSE	LOSE	SOUL	MILK	______	SOAR
53	KIND	DICE	LACE	WASP	______	MIST
54	PEAK	PEAT	MEAT	WAIT	______	HIVE
55	WROTE	LOWER	RELAY	VEINS	______	LARCH

5

Add one letter to the word in capital letters to make a new word. The meaning of the new word is given in the clue.

B 12

Example PLAN simple plain

56 HARE split, divide ______

57 TRUST drive, force ______

58 VICE human sound ______

59 CLAN washed ______

60 SIFT rapid ______

5

Fill in the missing letters. The alphabet has been written out to help you.

B 23

A B C D E F G H I J K L M N O P Q R S T U V W X Y Z

Example AB is to CD as PQ is to RS.

61 CF is to EH as RU is to ______.

62 VX is to UY as DG is to ______.

63 TW is to VZ as LP is to ______.

64 JK is to HI as ST is to ______.

65 SW is to VU as OG is to ______.

5

Underline the two words, one from each group, which are closest in meaning.

B 3

Example (race, shop, start) (finish, begin, end)

66 (justify, question, right) (legal, explain, penalty)

67 (rare, common, unusual) (sense, real, ordinary)

68 (tap, liquid, flood) (drought, overflow, trickle)

69 (stale, processed, cooked) (raw, old, fresh)

70 (mess, lose, wreck) (destroy, ship, save)

5

Move one letter from the first word and add it to the second word to make two new words.

B 13

Example hunt sip hut snip

71 fable lie ______ ______

72 port fail ______ ______

73 stable rush ______ ______

74 craft up ______ ______

75 grain net ______ ______

5

Write these words in alphabetical order.

B 20

76	artificial	artistic	artful	arrogant	arrest
	______	______	______	______	______
77	expand	exhilarate	expectancy	exile	exhibit
	______	______	______	______	______
78	recite	rebel	reason	reassure	rebuild
	______	______	______	______	______
79	illusion	illegible	illogical	illicit	illustrate
	______	______	______	______	______
80	foreign	forcible	forever	forecast	force
	______	______	______	______	______

5

Now go to the Progress Chart to record your score! Total 80

Paper 11

Change the first word into the last word by changing one letter at a time and making two new, different words in the middle.

B 13

Example	TEAK	TEAT	TENT	RENT
1	FIRE	______	______	FALL
2	FISH	______	______	MUST
3	NEAR	______	______	SELL
4	KERB	______	______	HARD
5	LACE	______	______	VILE
6	RICE	______	______	FACT

6

Complete the following sentences by selecting the most sensible word from each group of words given in the brackets. Underline the words selected.

B 14

Example The (children, books, foxes) carried the (houses, books, steps) home from the (greengrocer, library, factory).

7 It's important to make sure that your (customer, visitor, pet) doesn't (drink, eat, work) too much and become (lazy, overweight, bossy).

8 People who (travel, shop, listen) through space in a (computer, TV, rocket) are called (hikers, astronauts, dreamers).

9 Tom's (friend, teacher, mother) wrote in his (card, invitation, report) that he must (learn, improve, spell) his handwriting.

10 Most of her birthday (presents, cake, cards) showed pictures of (cats, candles, toys), but her favourite animal is actually a (doll, dog, drawing).

4

Find a word that can be put in front of each of the following words to make new, compound words.

Example cast fall ward pour *down*

11 pad book paper worthy ______

12 come cast all grown ______

13 back bulb card light ______

14 room robe tub water ______

15 standing line ground foot ______

Find a word that is similar in meaning to the word in capital letters and that rhymes with the second word.

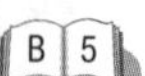

Example CABLE tyre *wire*

16 SWINDLE beat ______

17 STORY sail ______

18 PAINFUL moor ______

19 ARROW heart ______

20 MATCHED cared ______

Change the first word of the third pair in the same way as the other pairs to give a new word.

Example bind, hind bare, hare but, *hut*

21 tall, tail fall, fail wall, ______

22 risk, skin wish, shin bath, ______

23 net, nest pet, pest bet, ______

24 gape, page dame, made tame, ______

25 mare, ream name, mean post, ______

Complete the following expressions by underlining the missing word.

Example Frog is to tadpole as swan is to (duckling, baby, cygnet).

26 Wrist is to arm as ankle is to (foot, leg, toe).

27 Pleased is to delighted as solemn is to (tired, frightened, serious).

28 Sour is to sugary as reasonable is to (sensible, outrageous, thoughtful).

29 Fee is to cost as margin is to (paper, book, edge).

30 Clamour is to silence as readily is to (promptly, reluctantly, actually).

Fill in the crosswords so that all the given words are included. You have been given one letter as a clue in each crossword.

B 19

31–32

■		■		■	
					E
■		■		■	
■		■		■	

upside, meddle, spread,
riddle, advert, repeat.

33–34

■		■		■	
■		■		■	
■		■		■	
		P			

staple, stains, appear,
neatly, digest, osprey.

4

Here are the number codes for four words. Match the right code to the right word.

B 24

ECHO	COAL	HALO	LACE
4216	6145	3162	5432

35 ECHO ________

36 COAL ________

37 HALO ________

38 LACE ________

39 Write ACHE in code. ________

40 Write HOLE in code. ________

6

Give the two missing pairs of letters or numbers in the following sequences. The alphabet has been written out to help you with questions 41, 42 and 43.

B 23

A B C D E F G H I J K L M N O P Q R S T U V W X Y Z

Example	CQ	DP	EQ	FP	GQ	HP	
41	RD	___	TF	UG	VH	___	
42	CO	EM	GK	___	KG	___	
43	AV	BU	CT	___	___	FQ	
44	25	28	___	34	37	___	
45	52	57	54	59	___	___	

5

Underline the pair of words most similar in meaning.

B 5

Example come, go <u>roam, wander</u> fear, fare

46 attach, unfasten near, distant negotiate, discuss

47 waited, walked support, assist rapidly, slowly

48 peace, calm help, ignore cost, purse

49 graceful, clumsy gradual, immediate determined, persistent

4

Read the first two statements and then underline one of the four options below that must be true.

B 25

50 'Kumiko often goes to French Club on Saturday morning. Yesterday was Thursday.'

Kumiko enjoys learning French.

Kumiko is going to French Club today.

Tomorrow is Saturday.

French Club lasts for two hours.

1

Find two letters which will end the first word and start the second word.

B 10

Example rea (<u>c</u> <u>h</u>) air

51 ma (___ ___) elf

52 dra (___ ___) nage

53 enou (___ ___) ost

54 priva (___ ___) lephone

55 plea (___ ___) cond

5

Underline the one word in the brackets which will go equally well with both the pairs of words outside the brackets.

B 5

Example rush, attack cost, fee (price, hasten, strike, <u>charge</u>, money)

56 transport, aviation exit, fleeing (soaring, escape, trip, flight, aeroplane)

57 slim, slender prune, crop (neat, trim, compact, tidy, smart)

58 advert, flyer observe, see (paper, notice, look, read, say)

59 tie, stalemate trace, sketch (raffle, trace, skill, draw, prize)

60 express, show ventilate, freshen (appear, disclose, space, air, expose)

5

Underline the two words which are the odd ones out in the following groups of words.

B 4

Example	black	<u>king</u>	purple	green	<u>house</u>
61	disease	fever	nurse	infection	medicine
62	curiosity	involvement	boredom	concern	indifference
63	coffee	glass	juice	cup	milk
64	eat	chew	hunger	starving	munch
65	wings	robin	beak	ostrich	talon

5

Find the four-letter word which can be added to the letters in capitals to make a new word. The new word will complete the sentence sensibly.

B 22

Example They enjoyed the BCAST. ROAD

66 The bird was kept busy SEING for food and protecting the nest. ____________

67 The truck BED the road so no one could pass. ____________

68 He watched a very INTEING programme about dinosaurs. ____________

69 I REED the book to the library on time. ____________

70 It is IMANT to protect your skin when the sun is strong. ____________

5

Remove one letter from the word in capital letters to leave a new word. The meaning of the new word is given in the clue.

B 12

Example AUNT an insect ant

71 PAINTING breathless ____________

72 PASTRY small pie ____________

73 SPORT harbour ____________

74 SLIGHT glimpse ____________

75 QUIET give up ____________

5

Underline the two words which are made from the same letters.

B 7

Example	TAP	PET	<u>TEA</u>	POT	<u>EAT</u>	
76	REPEAT	TRAPPED	DEPART	TAPER	PARTED	DRAPE
77	DIME	MERIT	TIMED	METRE	REMIT	TREMOR
78	SEVER	SIEVE	SEVEN	VERSE	VEINS	NEVER
79	RETRACT	TRACER	RETRACE	CATERER	TRACTOR	REACT
80	HOSES	SHORT	HORSE	HORNS	SHOTS	SHORE

5

Now go to the Progress Chart to record your score! **Total** 80

Paper 12

Find the letter which will complete both pairs of words, ending the first word and starting the second. The same letter must be used for both pairs of words.

B 10

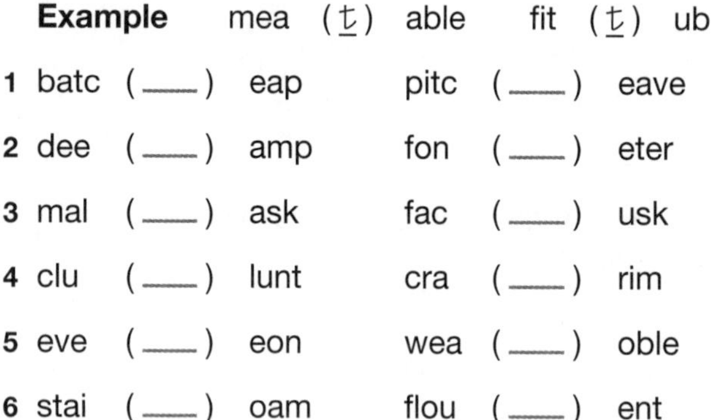

Example mea (t) able fit (t) ub

1 batc (__) eap pitc (__) eave

2 dee (__) amp fon (__) eter

3 mal (__) ask fac (__) usk

4 clu (__) lunt cra (__) rim

5 eve (__) eon wea (__) oble

6 stai (__) oam flou (__) ent

6

Spell the following words backwards. Write numbers underneath the words to indicate their new alphabetical order.

B 20

7 INVISIBLE IMPOSSIBLE INEDIBLE BUBBLE

______ ______ ______ ______

8 JUICE BRUISE CRUISE NUISANCE

______ ______ ______ ______

9 HOPING MAKING WAKING DRIVING

______ ______ ______ ______

3

Five friends, A, B, C, D and E are in a queue to buy tickets at the cinema.

A is not at the back of the queue and has one person in front of him.

E has three people ahead of him, and is standing in front of D.

B is at the front of the queue.

B 25

10 Which person is in the middle of the queue? ______

1

A B C D E F G H I J K L M N O P Q R S T U V W X Y Z

If A = 1, B = 2, C = 3 and so on, find the value of the following words by adding the letters together.

B 26

11 CAB ______

12 CAGE ______

13 BED ______

3

Fill in the crosswords so that all the given words are included. You have been given one letter as a clue in each crossword.

B 19

14–15

		W

wet, ewe, dog,
get, owe, dew

16–17

E		

era, urn, mad,
see, end, sum

4

A B C D E F G H I J K L M N O P Q R S T U V W X Y Z

If the code for COUNT is XLFMG, what are the codes for these words?

B 24

18 COT ________

19 NEAT ________

20 FISH ________

3

Underline the two words, one from each group, which are the most opposite in meaning.

B 9

Example (dawn, early, wake) (late, stop, sunrise)

21 (light, appear, view) (scenery, glow, vanish)

22 (type, sort, variety) (assortment, routine, different)

23 (ready, easily, gladly) (eager, unprepared, willingly)

24 (fee, jewel, treasured) (rich, ignored, cheap)

4

Read the first two statements and then underline one of the four options below that must be true.

B 25

25 'Most dogs wear a collar. Some collars have a name tag.'

All pets wear name tags.

Some dogs without collars might get lost.

Not all dogs have name tags.

Name tags are sold in pet shops.

1

Rearrange the muddled letters in capitals to make a proper word. The answer will complete the sentence sensibly.

B 16

Example A BEZAR is an animal with stripes. ZEBRA

26 The waiter will VERSE the coffee. ________

27 Let us UNTIE our forces. ________

28 Cameron DENSE to pass his swimming test. ________

29 Can you DEARTH the cotton through the needle? ________

30 Turn off the PALM before you go to sleep. ________

5

B 15

Complete the following sentences in the best way by choosing one word from each set of brackets.

Example Tall is to (tree, <u>short</u>, colour) as narrow is to (thin, white, <u>wide</u>).

31 First is to (early, number, beginning) as last is to (only, single, ending).

32 Frog is to (croaks, green, pond) as lion is to (cub, roars, kills).

33 Minimum is to (bad, least, maximum) as light is to (weight, heavy, load).

34 Child is to (children, play, school) as woman is to (dress, women, husband).

35 Dishonest is to (false, wrong, trustworthy) as protect is to (barrier, threaten, careful).

Look at the first group of three words. The word in the middle has been made from the other two words. Complete the second group of three words in the same way, making a new word in the middle.

Example	PA<u>IN</u>	INTO	<u>TO</u>OK	ALSO	<u>SOON</u>	ONLY
36	PINT	NAIL	PALE	TREE	________	TANK
37	RAMP	ROAM	BOAT	BULL	________	COIN
38	PURE	WIRE	WISP	YAWN	________	DOTE
39	CLOAK	MOLE	MODEL	WEIGH	________	THIRD
40	WEAN	SAFE	SELF	STOP	________	LEAF

Find the four-letter word which can be added to the letters in capitals to make a new word. The new word will complete the sentence sensibly.

Example They enjoyed the BCAST. <u>ROAD</u>

41 The wrecked car was AONED in the field. ________

42 Parents will be INED as soon as a decision is made. ________

43 Drive carefully past CYCS. ________

44 REING children for good behaviour is important. ________

45 They played BADON in the garden during the holiday. ________

Underline the two words which are the odd ones out in the following groups of words.

Example	black	<u>king</u>	purple	green	<u>house</u>
46	aeroplane	pilot	car	mechanic	engineer
47	lake	valley	plain	harbour	mountain
48	begin	suspend	terminate	start	discontinue
49	spiteful	cruel	compassionate	nasty	charitable
50	litter	rubbish	herd	insects	swarm

Change one word so that the sentence makes sense. Underline the word you are taking out and write your new word on the line.

B 14

Example I waited in line to buy a book to see the film. ticket

51 Writing in a dairy is a good way to remember special occasions. ________

52 When you are playing football, the aim is to score as many hits as possible. ________

53 Do not leave very young adults unsupervised with a dog. ________

54 You can use your dictionary to find out what a sum means. ________

55 A guinea pig is a small animal, often kept as a toy. ________

5

Add one letter to the word in capital letters to make a new word. The meaning of the new word is given in the clue.

B 12

Example PLAN simple plain

56 EXIT to be alive ________

57 STOKE pat gently ________

58 VALE worth ________

59 WARY tired ________

60 MINE cut into small pieces ________

5

Choose two words, one from each set of brackets, to complete the sentences in the best way.

B 15

Example Smile is to happiness as (drink, tear, shout) is to (whisper, laugh, sorrow).

61 Ideal is to perfect as (genuine, gentle, generous) is to (common, capable, calm).

62 Immense is to enormous as (cold, shivery, chilled) is to (hot, unfriendly, pleasant).

63 Sporty is to athlete as (clumsy, graceful, heavy) is to (plumber, ballerina, chef).

64 Ignore is to notice as (prevent, perform, plunge) is to (allow, check, block).

4

Here are the number codes for three words. Match the right code to the right word.

B 24

DEFY	OBEY	YEAR
8342	6472	2415

65 DEFY ________

66 OBEY ________

67 YEAR ________

Decode these numbers using the same code.

68 3862 ________

69 35416 ________

5

Fill in the missing letters. The alphabet has been written out to help you.

A B C D E F G H I J K L M N O P Q R S T U V W X Y Z

Example AB is to CD as PQ is to RS.

70 CXG is to DWH as HNA is to ______.

71 HEQ is to JGS as WRK is to ______.

72 BC is to YX as DE is to ______.

73 JFC is to IEB as OVK is to ______.

74 AD is to ZW as BE is to ______.

5

Give the two missing pairs of letters or numbers in the following sequences. The alphabet has been written out to help you.

A B C D E F G H I J K L M N O P Q R S T U V W X Y Z

Example	CQ	DP	EQ	FP	GQ	HP
75	AC	DF	___	JL	MO	___
76	___	DV	FT	HR	___	LN
77	VE	___	___	SH	RI	QJ
78	3	6	12	21	___	___
79	19	15	___	14	17	___
80	2	8	14	20	___	___

6

Now go to the Progress Chart to record your score! Total 80

Paper 13

Complete the following sentences in the best way by choosing one word from each set of brackets.

Example Tall is to (tree, short, colour) as narrow is to (thin, white, wide).

1 Complicated is to (wicked, tricky, straightforward) as loyal is to (faithful, difficult, awkward).

2 Prize is to (certificate, badge, reward) as penalty is to (punishment, gift, payment).

3 Exclude is to (allow, school, reject) as include is to (refuse, accept, destroy).

4 Bat is to (ball, wing, cricket) as rabbit is to (grass, hop, paw).

5 Imaginary is to (mind, possible, invented) as real is to (actual, copy, fake).

5

Remove one letter from the word in capital letters to leave a new word. The meaning of the new word is given in the clue.

B 12

Example	AUNT	an insect	ant
6	BEAN	forbid	______
7	HALVE	possess	______
8	SPLASH	cut	______
9	CARVE	hole under the ground	______
10	PATCH	course of action	______

5

Underline the two words, one from each group, which are closest in meaning.

B 3

Example	(race, shop, start)	(finish, begin, end)
11	(behave, reaction, move)	(response, look, knowledge)
12	(shorten, spread, lessen)	(traffic, expand, carry)
13	(arrange, definite, fix)	(harm, repair, vary)
14	(degree, lesser, deliberate)	(college, mistake, amount)
15	(spot, nest, hole)	(filling, opening, round)

5

Give the two missing numbers in the following sequences.

B 23

16	9	7	12	10	___	___	18
17	22	___	36	43	50	57	___
18	2	4	4	___	6	12	___
19	9	16	25	36	___	___	81
20	10	15	___	___	30	35	40

5

Claire and Amy are studying Science and Maths, and Harry and Fred study History and Geography.
Jacob and Henry like Art and Spanish, but Amelia's worst subject is French.
Ravi does Maths, but no longer has Geography lessons.
All the boys do Drama.

B 25

21 Which children are learning more than two subjects? ______

1

A B C D E F G H I J K L M N O P Q R S T U V W X Y Z

Solve the problems by working out the letter codes.

B 24

22 If the code for SOUP is VRXS, what is the code for SAVE? ______

23 If the code for FOLDER is HMNBGP, what is the code for MISTAKE? ______

24 If the code for BRAKE is DUEPK, what does the code YLRIE mean? ______

3

Read the first two statements and then underline one of the four options below that must be true.

B 25

25 'Crows and magpies are birds. Birds lay eggs.'

Magpies are black and white.

Crows lay eggs.

Many crows and magpies share nests.

Nests are only used for laying eggs.

1

Find two letters which will end the first word and start the second word.

B 10

Example rea (c h) air

26 almo (__ __) art

27 exci (__ __) mper

28 fra (__ __) lon

29 sha (__ __) rmit

30 whisp (__ __) upt

5

Find the missing number by using the two numbers outside the brackets in the same way as the other sets of numbers.

B 23

Example 2 [8] 4 3 [18] 6 5 [25] 5

31 6 [7] 9 8 [9] 11 10 [__] 13

32 7 [7] 49 9 [6] 54 4 [__] 32

33 12 [17] 22 16 [21] 26 2 [__] 12

34 9 [6] 7 10 [7] 8 12 [__] 10

35 24 [4] 6 36 [3] 12 27 [__] 3

5

Change the first word of the third pair in the same way as the other pairs to give a new word.

B 18

Example bind, hind bare, hare but, hut

36 hat, hatch mat, match pat, ______

37 bake, beak lake, leak wake, ______

38 trust, us clamp, am bring, ______

39 base, sea fear, are seat, ______

40 line, link tale, talk bare, ______

5

Underline the one word in the brackets which will go equally well with both the pairs of words outside the brackets.

B 5

Example	rush, attack	cost, fee	(price, hasten, strike, charge, money)
41	final, latest	continue, go on	(remain, last, cease, behind, proceed)
42	thorn, quill	annoy, pester	(tease, stick, needle, stem, poke)
43	earth, ground	arrive, come down	(planet, rest, soil, land, run)
44	explain, say	condition, phase	(report, shape, state, situation, express)
45	strong, firm	stern, strict	(solid, gentle, kind, healthy, tough)

5

Move one letter from the first word and add it to the second word to make two new words.

B 13

Example	hunt	sip	hut	snip
46	brisk	owl	______	______
47	brand	ham	______	______
48	flame	came	______	______
49	board	raw	______	______
50	tone	man	______	______

5

Give the two missing pairs of letters in the following sequences. The alphabet has been written out to help you.

B 23

A B C D E F G H I J K L M N O P Q R S T U V W X Y Z

Example	CQ	DP	EQ	FP	GQ	HP
51	DX	GU	JR	MO	___	___
52	BY	___	DW	EV	___	GT
53	WC	UE	VD	TF	___	___
54	___	OP	QR	ST	___	WX

4

Here are the number codes for four words. Match the right code to the right word.

B 24

ROAD	REAL	DARE	OVER
5736	2463	6341	6542

55 REAL ______

56 ROAD ______

57 DARE ______

58 OVER ______

Decode these numbers using the same code.

59 56236 ______

60 26573 ______

6

Look at the first group of three words. The word in the middle has been made from the other two words. Complete the second group of three words in the same way, making a new word in the middle. B 18

Example	PAIN	INTO	TOOK	ALSO	SOON	ONLY
61	ARMY	RACE	CHEW	OPEN	______	SITS
62	SLAP	PALM	HELM	REEF	______	BARN
63	CHIRP	RICE	PRICE	ELDER	______	DIVER
64	REIN	NOTE	OTTER	REAP	______	INCH
65	GAME	ROAM	BORE	OVEN	______	FAST

5

Rearrange the letters in capitals to make another word. The new word has something to do with the first two words. B 16

Example	spot	soil	SAINT	STAIN
66	unkind	nasty	NAME	______
67	players	game	MEAT	______
68	brave	challenge	READ	______
69	celebrity	twinkling light	RATS	______
70	vibrate	thump	BROTH	______

5

Fill in the crosswords so that all the given words are included. You have been given one letter as a clue in each crossword. B 19

71–72

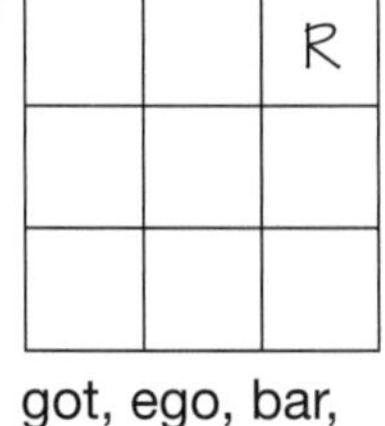

got, ego, bar, ago, rot, beg

73–74

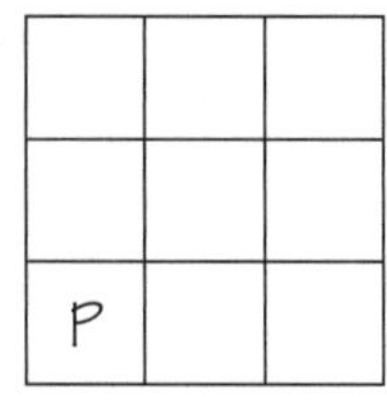

ace, net, tap, ice, pet, tin

4

Choose two words, one from each set of brackets, to complete the sentences in the best way. B 15

Example Smile is to happiness as (drink, tear, shout) is to (whisper, laugh, sorrow).

75 Bee is to buzz as (pig, wolf, duck) is to (piglet, lake, howl).

76 Rear is to back as (grab, give, punch) is to (hold, snatch, kick).

77 Crude is to polite as (pile, crowded, sandy) is to (crushed, demolished, deserted).

78 Leaf is to leaves as (cup, eyesight, glass) is to (water, glasses, mugs).

79 Tease is to irritate as (damage, assist, know) is to (harm, ignore, repair).

80 Star is to sky as (sail, wave, greeting) is to (friendly, land, sea).

6

Now go to the Progress Chart to record your score! Total 80

Progress Chart Verbal Reasoning 10–11^{+} years Book 2

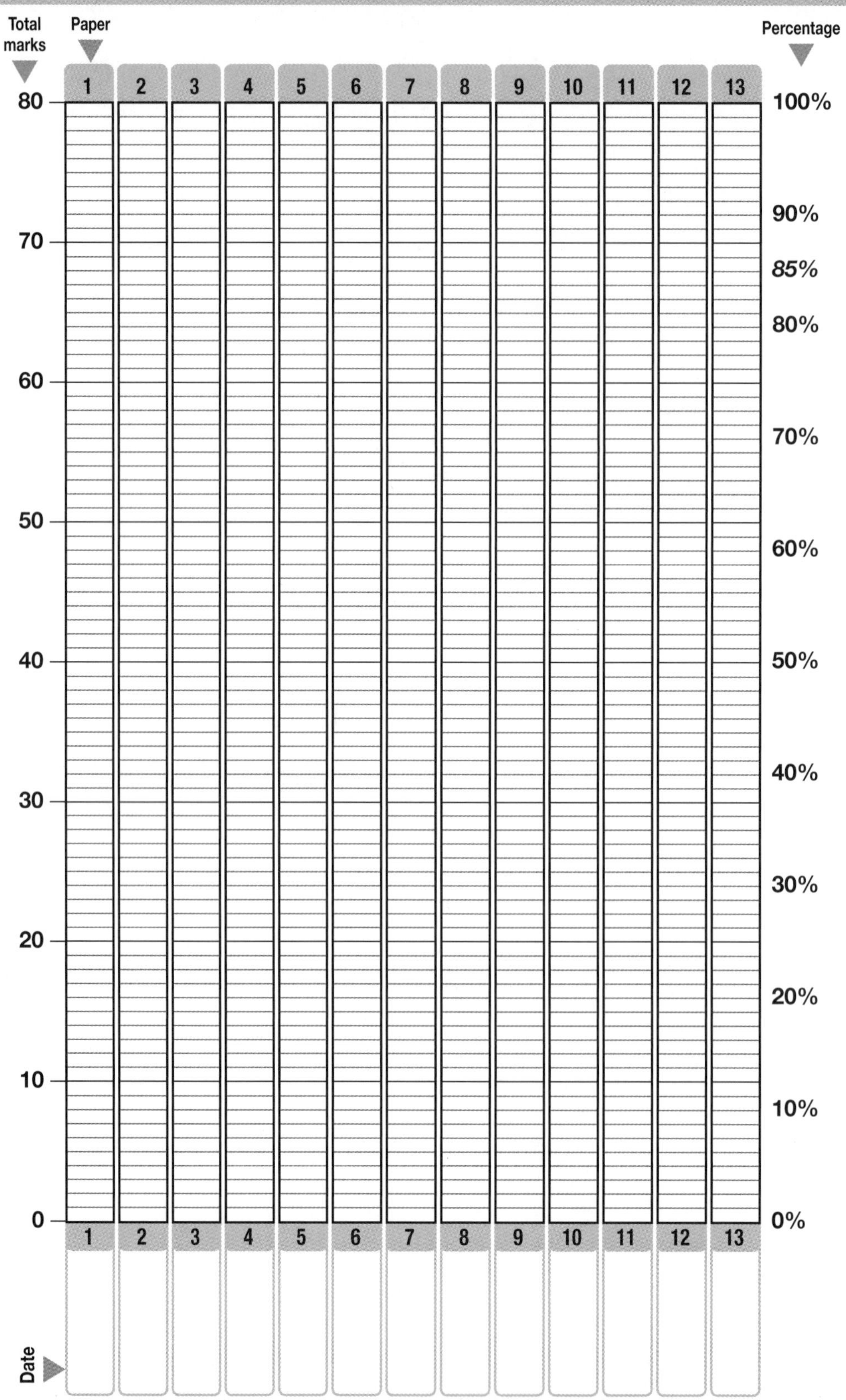

When you've finished the book use the Next Steps Planner